W9-BWC-441

BIG
BAD-ASS
BOOK OF
COCKTAILS

BIG

BAD-ASS

BOOK OF

COCKTAILS

1,500 RECIPES TO MIX IT UP!

BY PAUL KNORR

RUNNING PRESS
PHILADELPHIA · LONDON

9 8 7 6 5 4 3 2 1
Digit on the right indicates the number of this printing

Library of Congress Control Number: 2009934052

ISBN 978-0-7624-3839-6

Designed by Joshua McDonnell
Edited by Cindy De La Hoz
Typography: Bembo, Block, and Gill Sans

Running Press Book Publishers
2300 Chestnut Street
Philadelphia, PA 19103-4371

Visit us on the web!
www.runningpress.com

TABLE OF CONTENTS

537 Strawberry Bubble Bath
537 Strawberry Buttermilk
538 Strawberry Caipirinha
538 Strawberry Cake
538 Strawberry Daiquiri
539 Strawberry Girl
539 Strawberry Kir Royale
540 Strawberry Margarita
540 Strawberry Shortcake
541 Strawberry Sour
541 Strawberry Sunrise
541 Strawcherry
542 Street Scene
542 Stretcher Bearer
542 Stupid Cupid
543 Sue Riding High
543 Suede Vixen
543 Sugar Daddy
544 Suicide
544 Sumatra Juice
544 Summer Breeze
545 Summer Shade
545 Sun and Fun
545 Sun Deck
546 Sun of a Beach
546 Sunburn

546 Sundown
547 Sunny Beach
547 Sunny Island
547 Sunset Beach
548 Sunsplash
548 Super Genius
548 Supercaipi
549 Surfer on Acid Cocktail
549 Surfside Swinger
549 Surprise
550 Suze Tropic
550 Swamp Water
550 Sweat Heat
551 Swedish Fish
551 Swedish Lady
551 Sweet and Blue
552 Sweet Charge
552 Sweet Concoction
552 Sweet Dream Cocktail
553 Sweet Dumbo
553 Sweet Eden
553 Sweet Flamingo
554 Sweet Harmony
554 Sweet Smell of Success
554 Sweet Talker
555 Sweet Tart

'57 CHEVY

1 part Southern Comfort®
1 part gin
1 part vodka
Splash of orange juice
Splash of pineapple juice
Splash of grenadine
Shake Southern Comfort®, gin, vodka, orange juice, and
pineapple juice with ice and strain into a cocktail glass.
Top with grenadine.

'57 T-BIRD WITH FLORIDA PLATES

4 parts orange juice

1 part vodka

1 part triple sec

1 part Amaretto

Garnish: orange slice and cherry

Build on ice in a tall glass and stir.

Garnish with orange slice and cherry.

'57 T-BIRD WITH CALIFORNIA PLATES

4 parts grapefruit juice

1 part vodka

1 part triple sec

1 part Amaretto

Garnish: orange slice and cherry

Build on ice in a tall glass and stir.

Garnish with orange slice and cherry.

'57 T-BIRD WITH CAPE COD PLATES

4 parts cranberry juice
1 part vodka
1 part triple sec
1 part Amaretto
Garnish: lime wedge
Build on ice in a tall glass and stir.
Garnish with lime wedge.

'57 T-BIRD WITH HAWAIIAN PLATES

4 parts pineapple juice
1 part vodka
1 part triple sec
1 part Amaretto
Garnish: pineapple wedge
Build on ice in a tall glass and stir.
Garnish with pineapple wedge.

'81 CAMARO

2 parts vodka

1 part cola

1 part orange soda

3 scoops of vanilla ice cream

Mix in a blender and pour into a highball glass.

24K NIGHTMARE

1 part Goldschläger®

1 part Jägermeister®

1 part Rumple Minze®

1 part Bacardi 151®

Shake with ice and strain into a cocktail glass.

3 BANANAS

1 part banana vodka

1 part crème de banana

1 part banana juice

Shake with ice and strain into a cocktail glass.

3AM ON A SCHOOL NIGHT

3 parts fruit punch

1 part bourbon

Shake with ice and strain into a cocktail glass.

3RD STREET PROMENADE

2 parts vanilla vodka

1 part gin

1 part cinnamon schnapps

1 part orange juice

Shake with ice and strain into a cocktail glass.

57 MAGNUM

3 parts scotch

1 part triple sec

Dash of bitters

Garnish: orange slice

Shake with ice and strain into a cocktail glass. Garnish
with orange slice.

7 & 7

2 parts 7 Up®
1 part Seagram's 7®
Build on ice in a highball glass.

7 MILES

3 parts champagne
1 part pear juice
Splash of grenadine
Pour into a champagne flute and stir.

8TH WONDER

2 parts white wine
1 part brandy
1 part sour mix
Pour into a wine glass and stir.

9 1/2 WEEKS

2 parts Absolut® Citron
1 part blue curaçao
1 part orange juice
Splash of strawberry liqueur
Garnish: sliced strawberry
Shake with ice and strain into a cocktail glass. Garnish
with sliced strawberry.

ACAPULCO SUN

2 parts tequila
1 part Grand Marnier®
1 part sour mix
Shake with ice and strain into a cocktail glass.

ACE

2 parts pineapple juice
2 parts orange juice
1 part vodka
1 part lime juice (freshly squeezed)
Splash of grenadine
Pinch of sugar
Build on ice in a tall glass and stir.

ADONIS COCKTAIL

1 part sherry
Splash of sweet vermouth
Dash of bitters
Shake with ice and strain into a cocktail glass.

ADULT HOT COCOA

3 parts hot cocoa
1 part peppermint schnapps
Garnish: whipped cream
Shake and strain into a cocktail glass.
Garnish with whipped cream.

AFFINITY COCKTAIL

1 part scotch
1 part sweet vermouth
Dash of dry vermouth
Dash of bitters
Shake with ice and strain into a cocktail glass.

AFTER PARTY

2 parts vodka
1 part ginger ale
1 part pineapple juice
1 part cranberry juice
Pinch of sugar
Build on ice in a highball glass and stir.

AFTERBURNER

1 part Kahlua®
1 part Jägermeister®
Splash of Bacardi® 151
Shake with ice and strain into a cocktail glass.

AFTERGLOW

2 parts cream
1 part blueberry vodka
1 part advocaat
1 part orange juice
Build on ice in a highball glass and stir.

AFTERNOON PLEASURE

2 parts sweet vermouth
2 parts Amaretto
1 part orange juice
Shake with ice and strain into a cocktail glass.

ALABAMA SLAMMER COCKTAIL

2 parts orange juice
1 part Southern Comfort®
1 part Amaretto
1 part sloe gin
Shake with ice and strain into a cocktail glass.

ALASKAN MONK

1 part Frangelico®
1 part Bailey's Irish Cream®
1 part chocolate milk
Shake with ice and strain into a cocktail glass.

ALASKAN POLAR BEAR HEATER

2 parts vodka
1 part rum
1 part apple cider
Dash of dry vermouth
Shake with ice and strain into a cocktail glass.

ALBUQUERQUE ROYALE

3 parts cranberry juice

2 parts tequila

1 part triple sec

1 part sour mix

Build on ice in a tall glass and stir.

ALEXANDER

2 parts cream

1 part brown crème de cacao

1 part gin

Garnish: ground nutmeg

Shake with ice and strain into a cocktail glass. Garnish
with ground nutmeg.

ALIEN SECRETION

1 part Malibu Coconut Rum®

1 part melon liqueur

Splash of pineapple juice

Shake with ice and strain into a rocks glass.

ALIEN URINE

3 parts sour mix
3 parts orange juice
2 parts coconut rum
1 part Midori®
Build on ice in a tall glass and stir.

ALMA DE MINT

1 part Jose Cuervo® tequila
Splash of green crème de menthe
Splash of grapefruit juice
Splash of sour mix
Garnish: lime slice
Shake with ice and strain into a cocktail glass. Garnish with lime slice.

ALMA DE ROSA

2 parts dark rum

2 parts vanilla liqueur

1 part triple sec

1 part crème de banana

Splash of pineapple juice

Shake with ice and strain into a cocktail glass.

ALMOND AMARETTO FREEZE

1 part Amaretto

1 part cream

2 scoops of vanilla ice cream

Handful of almonds

Mix with ice in a blender and pour into a
highball glass.

ALMOND JOEY

3 parts Amaretto
1 part coconut milk
1 part chocolate syrup
3 scoops of vanilla ice cream
Mix with ice in a blender and pour into a highball glass.

ALMOND JOY

3 parts cream
1 part brown crème de cacao
1 part Amaretto
1 part coconut milk
Shake with ice and strain into a cocktail glass.

AMARETTO FLIRT

1 part sparkling wine
Splash of Amaretto
Splash of orange juice
Pour into a wine glass and stir.

AMARETTO SOUR

2 parts sour mix
1 part Amaretto
Garnish: orange slice and cherry
Shake with ice and strain into a rocks glass. Garnish
with orange slice and cherry.

AMERICAN BEAUTY SPECIAL

1 part blue curaçao
1 part Cognac
1 part rum
Garnish: lime wedge
Shake with ice and strain into a cocktail glass. Garnish
with lime wedge.

ANGEL FACE

2 parts gin

1 part apricot brandy

1 part apple brandy

Splash of pineapple juice

Stir with ice and strain into a cocktail glass.

ANIMAL ATTACK

2 parts Tanquerary® Ten

1 part Cointreau®

1 part peppermint schnapps

Splash of soda

Splash of lime juice (freshly squeezed)

Garnish: lime wedge

Build on ice in a highball glass and stir.

Garnish with lime wedge.

APPLE BLOW FIZZ

3 parts apple brandy

2 parts soda

1 egg white

Splash of lemon juice

Shake with ice and strain into a cocktail glass.

APPLE COOLNESS

2 parts apple cider

1 part coconut rum

Shake with ice and strain into a cocktail glass.

APPLE MARTINI

3 parts vodka

1 part apple schnapps

Garnish: cherry

Stir with ice and strain into a cocktail glass.

Garnish with cherry.

APPLE ORCHARD

2 parts tonic water
2 parts apple juice
1 part Apfelkorn
1 part apple brandy
Shake with ice and strain into a cocktail glass.

APPLE SAUCE

2 parts spiced rum
1 part sour mix
1 part apple cider
Splash of triple sec
Build on ice in a highball glass and stir.

APPLE SLUT

2 parts apple schnapps
1 part Absolut® Citron
1 part soda
Shake with ice and strain into a cocktail glass.

APPLE-CHEERYTINI

3 parts vodka
1 part apple schnapps
Garnish: apple slice
Shake with ice and strain into a cocktail glass. Garnish
with apple slice.

APRICOT COLA

3 parts apricot brandy
1 part cola
Splash of grenadine
Garnish: cherry
Shake with ice and strain into a cocktail glass. Garnish
with cherry.

APRICOT MARTINI

1 part gin
1 part apricot brandy
Splash of dry vermouth
Splash of lemon juice
Stir with ice and strain into a cocktail glass.

AQUA MARINA

2 parts champagne
1 part vodka
1 part peppermint schnapps
Pour into a wine glass and stir.

AS YOU WISH

2 parts amaro
1 part triple sec
1 part banana juice
Shake with ice and strain into a cocktail glass.

ASS-SMACKER

2 parts dark rum
2 parts cola
1 part white crème de menthe
Shake with ice and strain into a cocktail glass.

AT DAWN COCKTAIL

2 parts dark rum
2 parts Malibu Coconut Rum®
1 part blackberry schnapps
1 part pineapple juice
Shake with ice and strain into a cocktail glass.

AT SUNDOWN

2 parts brandy
1 part Vandermint®
Splash of lemon juice
Shake with ice and strain into a cocktail glass.

AT THE PARK

2 parts Bacardi® Gold Reserve
1 part triple sec
1 part apricot brandy
Splash of lime juice (freshly squeezed)
Shake with ice and strain into a cocktail glass.

AUNTIE'S CHOCOLATE

1 part Tia Maria®
1 part white crème de cacao
Shake with ice and strain into a cocktail glass.

AUTUMN FRUIT

2 parts vodka
1 part crème de banana
1 part dark rum
1 part strawberry liqueur
Shake with ice and strain into a cocktail glass.

AVALANCHE

3 parts advocaat
1 part apricot brandy
1 part apricot juice
2 scoops of vanilla ice cream
Mix with ice in a blender and pour
into a highball glass.

B-53

2 parts Kahlua®
1 part Amaretto
1 part Bailey's Irish Cream®
Shake with ice and strain into a rocks glass.

BACK AND FORTH

2 parts cream
1 part brown crème de cacao
1 part root beer schnapps
Shake with ice and strain into a cocktail glass

BAG OF TRICKS

1 part Cognac
1 part raspberry liqueur
Garnish: orange slice
Shake with ice and strain into a cocktail glass. Garnish
with orange slice.

BAHAMA MAMA

3 parts orange juice
3 parts pineapple juice
1 part light rum
1 part Malibu Coconut Rum®
1 part crème de banana
1 part grenadine
Garnish: pineapple wedge
Build on ice in a tall glass and stir. Garnish with pineapple wedge.

BAJA CALIFORNIA DREAM

3 parts tequila

Splash of sweet vermouth

Splash of dry vermouth

Garnish: cherry

Shake with ice and strain into a cocktail glass. Garnish with cherry.

BAJA FRUIT COCKTAIL

2 parts tequila

1 part plum brandy

1 part pineapple juice

1 part cranberry juice

Shake with ice and strain into a cocktail glass.

BAJA MARGARITA

2 parts tequila

2 parts lemonade

1 part blue curaçao

Shake with ice and strain into a cocktail glass.

BALALAIKA

3 parts white wine
1 part lemonade
1 part sloe gin
Pour into a wine glass and stir.

BALL BUSTER

2 parts beer
1 part whiskey
1 part Amaretto
1 part cola
Pour into a highball glass and stir.

BALLET RUSSE

3 parts vodka
1 part crème de cassis
Splash of lime juice
Shake with ice and strain into a cocktail glass.

BAMBOLEO PAPA SHAKE

3 parts Aperol
1 part dark rum
1 part pineapple juice
Splash of coconut cream
Splash of grenadine
Shake with ice and strain into a cocktail glass.

BAMBOO

1 part dry vermouth
1 part sherry
Shake with ice and strain into a cocktail glass.

BANANA BANSHEE

1 part white crème de cacao
1 part crème de banana
1 banana
3 scoops of vanilla ice cream
Mix in a blender and pour into a highball glass.

BANANA BLISS

1 part crème de banana
1 part Cognac
Shake with ice and strain into a cocktail glass.

BANANA BLUE HAWAIIAN

1 part rum
1 part blue curaçao
1 part pineapple juice
1 part guava juice
Shake with ice and strain into a cocktail glass.

BANANA BRACER

2 parts crème de banana
2 parts pineapple juice
2 parts orange juice
1 part apricot brandy
1 part cherry brandy
Build on ice in a highball glass and stir.

BANANA CHI CHI

1 part vodka
1 part crème de banana
1 part cranberry juice
1 part pineapple juice
1 part orange juice
Build on ice in a highball glass and stir.

BANANA COLADA

2 parts coconut rum
1 part banana vodka
1 part cream
Shake with ice and strain into a cocktail glass.

BANANA DREAM

1 part vodka
1 part banana liqueur
1 part white wine
1 part orange juice
Shake with ice and strain into a cocktail glass.

BANANA GIRL

1 part white crème de cacao
1 part Pisang Ambon®
1 part advocaat
1 part pineapple juice
Shake with ice and strain into a cocktail glass.

BANANA MUD PIE

2 parts banana vodka
1 part sambuca
1 part brown crème de cacao
1 part cream
Shake with ice and strain into a cocktail glass.

BANANA SPARKLER

2 parts sparkling wine
1 part crème de banana
1 part grapefruit juice
Pour into a champagne flute.

BANANA SURFER

3 parts white wine
1 part Frangelico®
1 part crème de banana
Pour into a wine glass and stir.

BANANAFANA

2 parts Aperol
1 part crème de banana
1 part white crème de cacao
1 egg white
Shake with ice and strain into a cocktail glass.

BANDIT'S COCKTAIL

1 part brandy
1 part brown crème de cacao
1 part butterscotch schnapps
Shake with ice and strain into a cocktail glass.

BANSHEE

2 parts cream
1 part white crème de cacao
1 part crème de banana
Shake with ice and strain into a cocktail glass.

BAY BREEZE

1 part vodka
1 part cranberry juice
1 part pineapple juice
Build on ice in a highball glass.

BEACH BABY

2 parts rum
1 part pineapple juice
1 part orange juice
1 part grenadine
Build on ice in a highball glass and stir.

BEACH COOLER

3 parts papaya juice
1 part vodka
Splash of Bacardi 151®
Shake with ice and strain into a cocktail glass.

BEER TOP

2 parts beer
1 part melon liqueur
1 part cranberry juice
Build on ice in a highball glass and stir.

BELLINI

3 parts champagne
1 part peach schnapps
Pour into a champagne flute.

BELOW THE EQUATOR

3 parts tequila

1 part tonic water

Splash of Galliano®

Shake tequila and tonic water with ice and strain into a
cocktail glass. Top with Galliano®.

BENEATH THE BLANKET

2 parts hot cocoa

1 part butterscotch schnapps

1 part cinnamon schnapps

Splash of vodka

Pour into an Irish coffee glass and stir.

BERRY MARGARITA

3 parts tequila

1 part strawberry liqueur

1 part triple sec

Splash of lime juice

Shake with ice and strain into a cocktail glass.

BERRY PLEASANT

2 parts strawberry milk
1 part coffee liqueur
1 part strawberry liqueur
1 part butterscotch schnapps
Build on ice in a highball glass and stir.

BEST IN SHOW

1 part dark rum
1 part apricot brandy
1 part cola
Splash of grenadine
Shake with ice and strain into a cocktail glass.

BETRAYED

2 parts gin
1 part white wine
1 part apple brandy
Splash of Frangelico®
Splash of blue curaçao
Garnish: lemon twist
Stir with ice and strain into a cocktail glass. Garnish
with lemon twist.

BEWITCHED

3 parts Strega®
1 part white crème de cacao
Splash of cream
Shake with ice and strain into a cocktail glass.

BIMBO

2 parts cranberry juice

1 part vodka

1 part triple sec

Splash of orange juice

Shake with ice and strain into a cocktail glass.

BITCH SLAP

2 parts cream

1 part Kahlua®

1 part Chambord®

Shake with ice and strain into a cocktail glass.

BITTER BAMBOO

3 parts sherry

Dash of dry vermouth

Dash of bitters

Shake with ice and strain into a cocktail glass.

COCOA NIGHTCAP

1 part Cognac
1 part Bénédictine
1 part brown crème de cacao
Shake with ice and strain into a cocktail glass.

COCO-NUT

2 parts brandy
1 part Malibu Coconut Rum®
1 part crème de noyaux
Shake with ice and strain into a cocktail glass.

COCONUT CREAM

2 parts crème de banana
1 part coconut rum
1 part grenadine
1 part cream
Shake with ice and strain into a cocktail glass.

COCONUT DAIQUIRI

2 parts coconut liqueur
1 part rum
1 part lime juice (freshly squeezed)
1 egg white
Shake with ice and strain into a cocktail glass.

COFFEE COLA

2 parts Kahlua®
1 part light rum
1 part cola
Shake with ice and strain into a cocktail glass.

COFFEE FRAISE

3 parts Bailey's Irish Cream®
1 part white crème de cacao
1 part strawberry milk
Splash of grenadine
Garnish: strawberry
Shake with ice and strain into a cocktail glass.
Garnish with strawberry.

COFFEE RUN

3 parts dark rum
1 part Tia Maria®
1 part cream
Garnish: cherry
Shake with ice and strain into a cocktail glass. Garnish
with cherry.

COLOMBIAN MONK

3 parts Frangelico®
1 part espresso
Garnish: scoop of vanilla ice cream
Pour into a highball glass.
Top with scoop of vanilla ice cream.

COLONEL COLLINS

3 parts sour mix
2 parts bourbon
1 part soda
Garnish: orange slice and cherry
Build on ice in a tall glass and stir.
Garnish with orange slice and cherry.

COLONEL'S CHOICE

1 part bourbon
1 part pastis
Splash of sweet vermouth
Dash of bitters
Shake with ice and strain into a cocktail glass.

COLONEL'S COFFEE

3 parts bourbon
1 part Kahlua®
1 part cola
Shake with ice and strain into a cocktail glass.

COLORADO BULLDOG

3 parts vodka
1 part Kahlua®
Splash of cream
Splash of cola
Build on ice in a rocks glass.

COMBAT JUICE

2 parts grape vodka
1 part raspberry liqueur
1 part grapefruit juice
Shake with ice and strain into a cocktail glass.

COME CLOSER

2 parts gin
1 part triple sec
1 part crème de banana
1 part Passoã®
1 tablespoon of strawberry syrup
Stir with ice and strain into a cocktail glass.

COMFORTABLE NUT

2 parts cola
1 part Southern Comfort®
1 part Amaretto
Splash of vodka
Shake with ice and strain into a cocktail glass.

CONCORD COCKTAIL

2 parts grape vodka
1 part white grape juice
Splash of cranberry juice
Garnish: red grape
Shake with ice and strain into a cocktail glass. Garnish
with red grape.

COSMOPOLITAN

3 parts vodka
1 part Cointreau®
Splash of lime juice
Splash cranberry juice
Garnish: lime wedge

Shake with ice and strain into a cocktail glass. Garnish with lime wedge.

COULD BE PARADISE

1 part vodka
1 part raspberry liqueur
1 part triple sec
1 part orange juice
Splash of Campari®

Shake with ice and strain into a cocktail glass.

COW COCKTAIL

2 parts whiskey
1 part white crème de cacao
1 part coffee
1 part condensed milk
1 egg white
2 scoops of vanilla ice cream
Splash of vanilla extract
Garnish: whipped cream
Mix with ice in a blender and pour into a
highball glass.

CRANBERRY MARGARITA

3 parts tequila
1 part Cointreau®
Splash of lime juice (freshly squeezed)
Splash of cranberry juice
Shake with ice and strain into a cocktail glass.

CRAN-MINT RUM

2 parts light rum
1 part cranberry juice
1 part peppermint schnapps
Garnish: mint sprig
Shake with ice and strain into a cocktail glass. Garnish
with mint sprig.

CRAZY FRENCHMAN

1 part apricot brandy
1 part pear brandy
Splash of sweet vermouth
Dash of bitters
Shake with ice and strain into a cocktail glass.

CREAMSICLE

2 parts cream
1 part white crème de cacao
1 part triple sec
1 part orange juice
Shake with ice and strain into a cocktail glass.

CREATIVITY

1 part black sambuca
1 part blackberry brandy
1 part Amaretto
1 part cream
Shake with ice and strain into a cocktail glass.

CREEPER

2 parts advocaat
1 part cherry schnapps
1 part pineapple juice
Shake with ice and strain into a cocktail glass.

CRIMEFIGHTER

2 parts gin
1 part pastis
Stir with ice and strain into a cocktail glass.

BLACK AND BLUE

1 part blackberry schnapps
1 part blue curaçao
1 part sour mix
Splash of soda
Shake with ice and strain into a cocktail glass.

BLACK CURRANT COGNAC

2 parts Cognac
1 part crème de cassis
1 part Bols® Vanilla
Shake with ice and strain into a cocktail glass.

BLACK LEGEND

2 parts champagne
1 part crème de cassis
1 part Campari®
Pour into a champagne flute.

BLACK MARTINI

1 part gin
Splash of crème de cassis
Garnish: black olive
Stir with ice and strain into a cocktail glass. Garnish
with black olive.

BLACK RUSSIAN

3 parts vodka
1 part Kahlua®
Build on ice in a rocks glass.

BLACK VODKA

2 parts crème de cassis
1 part vodka
Garnish: raspberries
Shake with ice and strain into a cocktail glass. Garnish
with raspberries.

BLACK WINDOWLESS VAN

4 parts dark rum
1 part raspberry liqueur
Splash of whiskey
Pinch of sugar
Shake with ice and strain into a cocktail glass.

BLACKBERRY BANDITO

1 part vodka
1 part blackberry schnapps
1 part lemonade
1 part orange juice
Shake with ice and strain into a cocktail glass.

BLACKBERRY MARGARITA

2 parts blackberry schnapps
1 part tequila
1 part triple sec
Shake with ice and strain into a cocktail glass.

BLAST OFF

1 part vodka
1 part Yukon Jack®
1 part peach schnapps
1 part cranberry juice
Shake with ice and strain into a cocktail glass.

BLIND SIDED

2 parts vodka
2 parts lemonade
1 scoop of vanilla ice cream
Garnish: lemon slice
Mix vodka, lemonade, and vanilla ice cream in blender
and pour into a highball glass.
Garnish with lemon slice.

BLIZZARD

4 parts gin
1 part sherry
1 scoop of vanilla ice cream
Mix in a blender and pour into a highball glass.

BLUE DEVIL

2 parts gin

1 part blue curaçao

1 part sour mix

Stir with ice and strain into a cocktail glass.

BLOODY GIN

1 part gin

Splash of hot sauce

Splash of lemon juice

Dash of salt

Garnish: celery stick

Stir with ice and strain into a cocktail glass.

BLOODY MARIA

2 parts Bloody Mary mix
(hot sauce, Worcestershire sauce, horseradish, tomato
juice, salt, and pepper)
1 part tequila
Garnish: celery stick
Build on ice in a highball glass. Garnish with
celery stick.

BLOODY MARY

2 parts Bloody Mary mix (hot sauce, Worcestershire
sauce, horseradish, tomato juice, salt, and pepper)
1 part vodka
Garnish: celery stick
Build on ice in a highball glass.
Garnish with celery stick.

BLOW ME

2 parts tequila

1 part brown crème de cacao

1 part cream

Garnish: chocolate powder

Shake with ice and strain into a cocktail glass.

Dust chocolate powder on top.

BLOWFISH

2 parts dark rum

1 part orange juice

1 part cranberry juice cocktail

1 part coconut cream

Build on ice in a highball glass and stir.

BLUE BALLS

2 parts grape juice

1 part vodka

1 part crème de noyaux

Shake with ice and strain into a cocktail glass.

BLUE CARNATION

2 parts cream
1 part white crème de cacao
1 part blue curaçao
Shake with ice and strain into a cocktail glass.

BLUE FLAMINGO

2 parts coconut liqueur
2 parts pineapple juice
1 part blue curaçao
Splash of strawberry liqueur
Build on ice in a highball glass and stir.

BLUE FOXTROT

2 parts light rum
1 part lemon juice
Splash of blue curaçao
Shake with ice and strain into a cocktail glass.

BLUE HAWAIIAN

3 parts pineapple juice

2 parts light rum

1 part blue curaçao

1 part soda

Garnish: pineapple wedge and cherry

Build on ice in a tall glass and stir. Garnish with
pineapple wedge and cherry.

BLUE IN THE FACE

1 part gin

1 part blue curaçao

1 part tonic water

Garnish: lemon slice

Stir with ice and strain into a cocktail glass. Garnish
with lemon slice.

BLUE ISLAND

2 parts cream

2 parts light rum

1 part blue curaçao

1 part vanilla liqueur

Shake with ice and strain into a cocktail glass.

BLUE KAMIKAZE COCKTAIL

3 parts vodka

1 part blue curaçao

1 part sour mix

Garnish: lemon slice

Shake with ice and strain into a cocktail glass.

Garnish with lemon slice.

BLUE MARGARITA

3 parts tequila

3 parts sour mix

1 part blue curaçao

1 part lime juice

Garnish: salt rim and lime wedge

Rim margarita glass with lime, then dip rim in salt.

Shake tequila, blue curaçao, lime juice, and sour mix
with ice and strain into the salt-rimmed glass.

Garnish with lime wedge.

BLUE MARTINI

1 part gin

Splash of blue curaçao

Garnish: orange twist

Stir with ice and strain into a cocktail glass. Garnish
with orange twist.

BLUE SLUSH PUPPY

1 part blue curaçao
1 part lemonade
Shake with ice and strain into a cocktail glass.

BLUE SPARKLER

2 parts sparkling wine
1 part gin
Splash of blue curaçao
Dash of bitters
Pour into a wine glass and stir.

BLUE VELVET

2 parts melon liqueur
2 parts apple juice
1 part blue curaçao
Shake with ice and strain into a cocktail glass.

BLUEBERRY MARTINI

1 part gin
Splash of Chambord®
Splash of blue curaçao
Stir with ice and strain into a cocktail glass.

BLUEBERRY SODA

3 parts blueberry vodka
1 part blueberry schnapps
1 part soda
Garnish: blueberries
Shake with ice and strain into a cocktail glass. Garnish
with blueberries.

BLUE-CRAN COLA

2 parts blueberry vodka
1 part cranberry juice
1 part cola
Garnish: blueberries
Shake with ice and strain into a cocktail glass.
Garnish with blueberries.

BLUSHIN' RUSSIAN

2 parts vodka
1 part cherry brandy
Shake with ice and strain into a cocktail glass.

BMW

1 part Bailey's Irish Cream®
1 part Malibu Coconut Rum®
1 part whiskey
Pour into a wine glass and stir.

BOCCE BALL

2 parts orange juice
1 part Amaretto
Build on ice in a highball glass.

BOMB ASS MIX

1 part scotch
1 part whiskey
1 part strawberry liqueur
Dash of bitters
Shake with ice and strain into a cocktail glass.

BOMBAY BANANA

2 parts Bombay Sapphire®
1 part triple sec
1 part crème de banana
Garnish: orange slice
Stir with ice and strain into a rocks glass. Garnish with
orange slice.

BORDERLINE

3 parts grape soda
1 part tequila
1 part vodka
1 part sloe gin
Splash of Bacardi 151®
Build on ice in a tall glass and stir.

BOTTOMS UP

1 part peach schnapps
1 part lemon-lime soda
Shake with ice and strain into a cocktail glass.

BOURBON SLUSH

1 part bourbon
Splash of lemonade
Pinch of sugar
Shake with ice and strain into a cocktail glass.

BRAIN COCKTAIL

3 parts strawberry liqueur
1 part Bailey's Irish Cream®
1 part grenadine
Shake with ice and strain into a cocktail glass.

BRAINIAC

2 parts banana juice
1 part light rum
1 part triple sec
Shake with ice and strain into a cocktail glass.

BRANDY ALEXANDER

2 parts cream
1 part brown crème de cacao
1 part brandy
Garnish: ground nutmeg
Shake with ice and strain into a cocktail glass. Garnish
with ground nutmeg.

BRANDYWINE

1 part apple brandy

1 part apricot brandy

Splash of pastis

Shake with ice and strain into a cocktail glass.

BRAZEN HUSSY

2 parts vodka

2 parts triple sec

Splash of lemon juice

Garnish: lemon wedge

Shake with ice and strain into a cocktail glass. Garnish
with lemon wedge.

BRAZIL NUT

2 parts cachaça
1 part lime juice
1 part pineapple juice
Pinch of brown sugar
Garnish: basil leaves

Shake with ice and strain into a cocktail glass. Garnish
with basil leaves.

BRAZILIAN APE

2 parts rum
1 part cachaça
1 part banana juice

Shake with ice and strain into a cocktail glass.

BREATHALYZER

2 parts orange juice
1 part Southern Comfort®
Splash of lemon–lime soda
Dash of Bacardi 151®
Shake with ice and strain into a cocktail glass.

BREATHLESS

2 parts white wine
1 part crème de banana
1 part Frangelico®
Pour into a champagne flute.

BRIDAL PARTY

1 part vodka
1 part cherry brandy
1 part Licor 43®
Splash of grenadine
Shake with ice and strain into a cocktail glass.

BRING IT ON

1 part Frangelico®
1 part Bailey's Irish Cream®
1 part Grand Marnier®
Splash of Kahlua®
Shake with ice and strain into a cocktail glass.

BUTTER 'N SPICE

1 part spiced rum
1 part butterscotch schnapps
1 part cream
Shake with ice and strain into a cocktail glass.

BUTTER UP

2 parts butterscotch schnapps
1 part crème de banana
1 part strawberry-kiwi juice
Shake with ice and strain into a cocktail glass.

BUTTERFLY

2 parts white wine
1 part advocaat
Splash of grenadine
Pour into a wine glass and stir.

BUTTERWORTH

2 parts Bailey's Irish Cream®
2 parts cream
1 part bourbon
Splash of Frangelico®
Shake with ice and strain into a cocktail glass.

BUTTERY NIPPLE COCKTAIL

3 parts butterscotch schnapps
3 parts cream
1 part Bailey's Irish Cream®
Shake with ice and strain into a cocktail glass.

BUTTMEISTER

2 parts Jägermeister

2 parts soda

1 part butterscotch schnapps

Shake with ice and strain into a cocktail glass.

BY MY SIDE

2 parts vodka

1 part sloe gin

1 part cranberry juice

Shake with ice and strain into a cocktail glass.

CACTUS BANGER

3 parts orange juice
1 part Mandarine Napoléon®
1 part tequila
Shake with ice and strain into a cocktail glass.

CACTUS BITE

1 part tequila
1 part lemonade
Splash of triple sec
Pinch of sugar
Dash of bitters
Shake with ice and strain into a cocktail glass.

CACTUS FLOWER

4 parts tequila
1 part blue curaçao
Splash of vanilla extract
Garnish: lime wedge
Shake with ice and strain into a cocktail glass. Garnish
with lime wedge.

CACTUS JACK

2 parts pineapple juice
2 parts orange juice
1 part cherry vodka
1 part blue curaçao
Build on ice in a highball glass and stir.

CACTUS VENOM

2 parts tequila
1 part Kahlua®
1 part white crème de cacao
Shake with ice and strain into a cocktail glass.

CAESAR COCKTAIL

3 parts vodka

1 part tomato juice

Dash of hot sauce

Dash of Worcestershire sauce

Shake with ice and strain into a cocktail glass.

CAFÉ DE PARIS COCKTAIL

1 part gin

1 egg white

Splash of cream

Splash of anisette

Stir with ice and strain into a cocktail glass.

CAFÉ KIRSCH COCKTAIL

2 parts gin

1 part Kirschwasser

1 egg white

Stir with ice and strain into a cocktail glass.

CAFÉ ROYALE FRAPPE

1 part brandy

1 part cold coffee

Shake with ice and strain into a cocktail glass.

CAFÉ TRINIDAD

1 part dark rum

1 part Tia Maria®

1 part cream

Dash of bitters

Shake with ice and strain into a cocktail glass.

CAFFEINATED

2 parts hot coffee

1 part coconut rum

1 part peach schnapps

Garnish: whipped cream

Pour into an Irish coffee glass and stir. Garnish with whipped cream.

CAKE-A-JAMAICA

2 parts dark rum
1 part triple sec
1 part brown crème de cacao
Garnish: whipped cream

Shake with ice and strain into a cocktail glass. Garnish with whipped cream.

CALEIGH

3 parts scotch
1 part blue curaçao
1 part white crème de cacao

Shake with ice and strain into a cocktail glass.

CALIFORNIA COASTLINE

3 parts pineapple juice

3 parts sour mix

1 part spiced rum

1 part peach schnapps

1 part blue curaçao

Build on ice in a tall glass and stir.

CALIFORNIA MARTINI

3 parts vodka

1 part red wine

Splash of dark rum

Shake with ice and strain into a cocktail glass.

CALL GIRL

4 parts orange juice
4 parts pineapple juice
1 part crème de banana
1 part light rum
1 part dark rum
1 part melon liqueur
1 part coconut liqueur
Build on ice in a tall glass and stir.

CALVADOS CREAM

2 parts advocaat
2 parts spiced rum
1 egg white
Shake with ice and strain into a cocktail glass.

CAMOUFLAGE CANNONBALL

3 parts sparkling wine

1 part light rum

1 part blue curaçao

Pinch of sugar

Garnish: chopped cucumber

Muddle sugar and cucumber in a wine glass. Pour in sparkling wine, light rum, and blue curaçao and stir.

CAMP GRENADA

3 parts lemon-lime soda

1 part Campari®

1 part Strega®

Build on ice in a highball glass and stir.

CAMPANILE

2 parts orange juice
1 part gin
1 part apricot brandy
1 part Campari®
Stir with ice and strain into a cocktail glass.

CAMPARI MARTINI

3 parts vodka
1 part Campari®
Shake with ice and strain into a cocktail glass.

CAMPAY

2 parts grapefruit juice
1 part gin
1 part Campari®
Pinch of sugar
Stir with ice and strain into a cocktail glass.

CANADA

3 parts whiskey

1 part triple sec

1 tablespoon of syrup

Dash of bitters

Shake with ice and strain into a cocktail glass.

CANADIAN BEAUTY

3 parts whiskey

1 part port wine

1 part orange juice

1 part peppermint schnapps

Shake with ice and strain into a cocktail glass.

CANDY

3 parts cranberry juice

1 part melon liqueur

1 part Amaretto

Garnish: orange slice and cherry

Build on ice in a tall glass and stir. Garnish with orange slice and cherry.

CANDY APPLE

1 part vodka
1 part apple schnapps
1 part grenadine
Garnish: cherry
Shake with ice and strain into a cocktail glass. Garnish with cherry.

CAPE CODDER

2 parts cranberry juice
1 part vodka
Garnish: lime wedge
Build on ice in a highball glass. Garnish with lime wedge.

CARAMEL APPLE

1 part dark rum
1 part apple schnapps
1 part caramel liqueur
Garnish: caramel syrup rim
Shake with ice and strain into a caramel-rimmed
cocktail glass.

CARAWAY COCKTAIL

1 part Kümmel
1 part gin
Splash of lime juice
Stir with ice and strain into a cocktail glass.

CARIBBEAN CRUISE

2 parts chocolate liqueur
2 parts pineapple juice
1 part Malibu Coconut Rum®
1 part crème de banana
Shake with ice and strain into a cocktail glass.

CARIBBEAN FRUIT ORGY

1 part light rum
1 part Apfelkorn
1 part orange juice
Splash of grenadine
Shake with ice and strain into a cocktail glass.

CARIOCA

1 part Bénédictine
1 part cherry brandy
Pour into a brandy snifter.

CASSIS VINE

2 parts cola
1 part grape vodka
Splash of crème de cassis
Garnish: cherry
Build on ice in a highball glass and stir. Garnish with
cherry.

CATCH ME IF YOU CAN

1 part Bailey's Irish Cream® Mint Chocolate

1 part vanilla vodka

1 part cream

Shake with ice and strain into a cocktail glass.

CAVALIER

2 parts Strega®

1 part peppermint schnapps

Shake with ice and strain into a cocktail glass.

CEASEFIRE

4 parts lemon-lime soda

1 part scotch

1 part dry vermouth

1 part cherry brandy

Build on ice in a highball glass and stir.

CELEBRATE LIFE

2 parts crème de banana
1 part triple sec
1 part vodka
Splash of orange juice
Shake with ice and strain into a cocktail glass.

CHAMELEON

1 part blue curaçao
1 part light rum
1 part orange juice
Shake with ice and strain into a cocktail glass.

CHAMPAGNE COCKTAIL

1 part champagne
1 tablespoon of sugar
Dash of bitters
Garnish: lemon twist
Muddle sugar and bitters in a
champagne flute. Pour champagne.
Garnish with lemon twist.

CHEESECAKE

2 parts vanilla vodka
2 parts cream
1 part triple sec
1 part white crème de cacao
Garnish: lemon wedge

Shake with ice and strain into a cocktail glass. Garnish with lemon wedge.

CHERRY BEER

1 part beer
1 part cherry cola
Garnish: cherry

Pour into a tall glass. Garnish with cherry.

CHERRY BOMB

3 parts Red Bull®
1 part cherry vodka
Pour into a highball glass.

CHERRY COLA

2 parts cola
1 part grenadine
Garnish: cherry
Build on ice in a highball glass.
Garnish with cherry.

CHERRY LIFESAVER COCKTAIL

3 parts Amaretto
1 part Southern Comfort®
1 part cranberry juice
1 part soda
Shake with ice and strain into a cocktail glass.

CHERRY POP

2 parts cream

1 part white crème de cacao

1 part maraschino liqueur

Garnish: cherry

Shake with ice and strain into a cocktail glass.

Garnish with cherry.

CHERRY SPARKLER

2 parts sparkling wine

1 part gin

1 part cherry schnapps

Pour into a wine glass and stir.

CHERRY TRUFFLE

2 parts chocolate milk
1 part cherry vodka
1 part coffee liqueur
1 part crème de banana
Garnish: cherry
Build on ice in a highball glass and stir.
Garnish with cherry.

CHERRY-RAZZ SOUR

2 parts sour mix
1 part cherry vodka
1 part raspberry liqueur
Shake with ice and strain into a cocktail glass.

CHI CHI

2 parts coconut milk
1 part vodka
1 part pineapple juice
Garnish: pineapple wedge and whipped cream
Mix coconut milk and vodka with ice in a blender and
pour into a glass. Garnish with pineapple wedge and
whipped cream.

CHOCKFULL

2 parts Amaretto
1 part cachaça
1 part chocolate liqueur
Garnish: cinnamon stick
Shake with ice and strain into a cocktail glass.
Garnish with cinnamon stick.

CHOCOLAT

2 parts light rum
1 part apricot brandy
Splash of Bols® Chocolate Mint
Shake with ice and strain into a cocktail glass.

CHOCOLATE CAKE

1 part vanilla vodka
1 part Frangelico®
Shake with ice and strain into a rocks glass.

CHOCOLATE CHERRY

1 part cherry vodka
1 part chocolate liqueur
1 part cola
Garnish: cherry
Shake with ice and strain into a cocktail glass.
Garnish with cherry.

CHOCOLATE COFFEE

2 parts cola
1 part chocolate liqueur
1 part coffee liqueur
1 part sloe gin
Shake with ice and strain into a cocktail glass.

CHOCOLATE GRASSHOPPER

2 parts chocolate milk
1 part green crème de menthe
1 part white crème de cacao
Shake with ice and strain into a cocktail glass.

CHOCOLATE MARTINI

3 parts vanilla vodka
1 part chocolate liqueur
Garnish: cherry
Stir with ice and strain into a cocktail glass.
Garnish with cherry.

CHOCOLATE MONKEY

1 part banana vodka

Splash of brown crème de cacao

Garnish: whipped cream

Shake with ice and strain into a cocktail glass.
Garnish with whipped cream.

CHOCOLATE SPICE

3 parts cream

2 parts coconut liqueur

2 parts coffee liqueur

1 part spiced rum

Splash of chocolate liqueur

Build on ice in a highball glass and stir.

CINNAMINNY

3 parts vodka

1 part cinnamon schnapps

Dash of dry vermouth

Shake with ice and strain into a cocktail glass.

CINNAMINT

2 parts cinnamon schnapps
1 part vanilla vodka
1 part green crème de menthe
1 part tonic water
Shake with ice and strain into a cocktail glass.

CINNAMON APPLE

2 parts cream
1 part Goldschläger®
1 part apple schnapps
Shake with ice and strain into a cocktail glass.

CITY SLICKER

4 parts brandy
1 part triple sec
Splash of lemon juice
Garnish: lemon wedge
Shake with ice and strain into a cocktail glass.
Garnish with lemon wedge.

CLAM UP

1 part gin
1 part tomato juice
Splash of hot sauce
Pour into a highball glass and stir.

CLEOPATRA COCKTAIL

2 parts tequila
1 part Bols® Bitter Orange
1 part mango juice
Splash of lemon juice
Shake with ice and strain into a cocktail glass.

CLIFFHANGER

2 parts light rum
1 part white crème de cacao
1 part blue curaçao
1 part cream
Shake with ice and strain into a cocktail glass.

CUBA LIBRE

2 parts cola
1 part light rum
Build on ice in a highball glass.

CURRANT SOUR

2 parts sour mix
1 part currant vodka
Splash of grenadine
Build on ice in a highball glass and stir.

CURTAIN CALL

1 part peppermint schnapps
1 part brown crème de cacao
1 part Frangelico®
1 part cream
Garnish: ground nutmeg
Shake with ice and strain into a cocktail glass.
Garnish with ground nutmeg.

DAILY DOUBLE C

1 part rum
1 part sweet vermouth
1 part maraschino liqueur
Garnish: cherry

Shake with ice and strain into a cocktail glass. Garnish with cherry.

DAIQUIRI

2 parts sour mix
1 part light rum

Shake with ice and strain into a rocks glass.

DAISY

1 part vodka

1 part peppermint schnapps

1 part triple sec

Dash of dry vermouth

Shake with ice and strain into a cocktail glass.

DAMN THE WEATHER MARTINI

1 part gin

Splash of sweet vermouth

Splash of orange juice

Splash of triple sec

Stir with ice and strain into a cocktail glass.

DANCE WITH A DREAM

4 parts brandy

1 part triple sec

Splash of anisette

Shake with ice and strain into a cocktail glass.

DAY AT THE BEACH

3 parts orange juice
1 part Malibu Coconut Rum®
Splash of Amaretto
Splash of grenadine
Garnish: pineapple wedge
Shake orange juice, Malibu Coconut Rum®, and
Amaretto with ice and strain into a cocktail glass. Float
grenadine on top. Garnish with pineapple wedge.

DAYDREAM

3 parts peach schnapps
1 part apple cider
Shake with ice and strain into a cocktail glass.

DEAN MARTINI

1 part gin

Splash of Aperol

Dash of bitters

Garnish: lemon twist

Stir with ice and strain into a cocktail glass. Garnish
with lemon twist.

DEATH FROM ABOVE

4 parts cola

1 part Bacardi 151®

Shake with ice and strain into a cocktail glass.

DEAUVILLE

1 part brandy

1 part apple brandy

1 part triple sec

Splash of lemon juice (freshly squeezed)

Shake with ice and strain into a cocktail glass.

DEBUTANTE'S DREAM

1 part coconut brandy
1 part orange juice
Splash of lime juice
Shake with ice and strain into a cocktail glass.

DEEP SEA COCKTAIL

1 part gin
1 part dry vermouth
Splash of anisette
Dash of bitters
Stir with ice and strain into a cocktail glass.

DEEP SEA MARTINI

3 parts gin
1 part apple juice
Splash of anisette
Stir with ice and strain into a cocktail glass.

DESERT DRY MARTINI

1 part gin

Garnish: olive

Stir with ice and strain into a cocktail glass. Garnish with olive.

DESERT FIRE

3 parts white grape juice

1 part tequila

1 part pastis

1 part triple sec

Splash of lime juice

Splash of hot sauce

Build on ice in a tall glass and stir.

DESIRE

1 part brown crème de cacao
1 part coffee liqueur
Splash of chocolate vodka
Garnish: chocolate rim
Shake with ice and strain into a
chocolate-rimmed cocktail glass.

DESSERT

2 parts light rum
1 part advocaat
Garnish: scoop of vanilla ice cream
Pour into a double rocks glass and stir.
Top with scoop of vanilla ice cream.

DEVIL COCKTAIL

1 part brandy

1 part sweet vermouth

Splash of blue curaçao

Dash of bitters

Garnish: cherry

Shake with ice and strain into a cocktail glass. Garnish with cherry.

DEVIL'S SMILE

1 part gin

1 part brandy

1 part triple sec

1 part lemonade

Dash of Amaretto

Stir with ice and strain into a cocktail glass.

DIFFERENCES

2 parts peach schnapps
2 parts Cognac
1 part Campari®
1 part peach juice
Shake with ice and strain into a cocktail glass.

DIRTY BASTARD

3 parts orange juice
2 parts peach schnapps
1 part vodka
Build on ice in a highball glass and stir.

DIRTY MARTINI

1 part gin
Splash of olive juice
Dash of dry vermouth
Garnish: 2 olives
Shake all ingredients, including garnish,
with ice and strain into a cocktail glass.

DIRTY MOTHER

3 parts brandy
1 part Kahlua®
Build on ice in a rocks glass.

DISCHARGED SOLDIER

3 parts Absolut® Citron
1 part blue curaçao
1 part apple juice
Garnish: lemon slice
Shake with ice and strain into a cocktail glass. Garnish
with lemon slice.

DIXIE COCKTAIL

1 part gin
Dash of dry vermouth
Dash of anisette
Splash of orange juice (freshly squeezed)
Stir with ice and strain into a cocktail glass.

DO ME JUICE

1 part gin

1 part cherry brandy

Dash of dry vermouth

Dash of bitters

Dash of lemon juice (freshly squeezed)

Stir with ice and strain into a cocktail glass.

DOCTOR

1 part gin

1 part fruit punch

1 part lemon juice

Stir with ice and strain into a cocktail glass.

DODGE EXPRESS

2 parts gin

1 part grape juice

Splash of soda

Stir with ice and strain into a cocktail glass.

DON'T BE BITTER

1 part vodka
1 part cinnamon schnapps
1 part cream
Splash of Amaretto
Shake with ice and strain into a cocktail glass.

DOSHA

2 parts applejack
1 part apricot brandy
1 part lemon juice
Shake with ice and strain into a cocktail glass.

DRAG

1 part Drambuie®
1 part Bailey's Irish Cream®
1 part brandy
Shake with ice and strain into a cocktail glass.

DREAM IN SCARLET

2 parts orange juice
1 part Bols® Red Orange
Splash of sweet vermouth
Shake with ice and strain into a cocktail glass.

DRUNKEN ELF

1 part white wine
1 part white crème de menthe
1 part cinnamon schnapps
Pour into a wine glass and stir.

DUBLIN DELIGHT

3 parts vodka
1 part Midori®
Splash of Amaretto
Garnish: cherry
Shake and strain into a rocks glass filled with ice.
Garnish with cherry.

DUSK TO DAWN

3 parts Bols® Genever
1 part raspberry liqueur
Splash of grenadine
Splash of lime juice (freshly squeezed)
Shake with ice and strain into a cocktail glass.

DUTCH VELVET

4 parts cream
1 part chocolate vodka
1 part banana vodka
1 part white crème de menthe
Garnish: shaved chocolate
Shake with ice and strain into a cocktail glass. Garnish
with shaved chocolate.

EARLY AFTERNOON

1 part Cognac
1 part green crème de menthe
1 part beer
Shake with ice and strain into a cocktail glass.

EARTH OF FIRE

2 parts grappa
1 part blue curaçao
Pinch of sugar
Garnish: lemon slice
Shake with ice and strain into a cocktail glass. Garnish
with lemon slice.

EARTHQUAKE

1 part whiskey

1 part gin

Shake with ice and strain into a cocktail glass.

EDIBLE PANTIES

2 parts dark rum

2 parts cola

1 part blackberry schnapps

Shake with ice and strain into a cocktail glass.

EL PRESIDENTE

1 part rum

Splash of grenadine

Splash of pineapple juice

Splash of lime juice

Shake with ice and strain into a cocktail glass.

ELATION

3 parts light rum
1 part caramel liqueur
1 part vanilla liqueur
Shake with ice and strain into a cocktail glass.

ELECTRIC LEMONADE

4 parts sour mix
1 part gin
1 part vodka
1 part rum
1 part tequila
1 part triple sec
1 part soda
Garnish: lemon wedge
Build on ice in a tall glass and stir. Garnish with lemon
wedge.

ELECTRIC WATERMELON

4 parts sour mix
1 part vodka
1 part light rum
1 part Midori®
1 part triple sec
Splash of club soda
Splash of Grenadine
Build on ice in a highball glass and stir.

ELEPHANT LIPS

3 parts dark rum
1 part crème de banana
Splash of lemon juice
Shake with ice and strain into a cocktail glass.

E-MAIL

1 part coffee liqueur

1 part Cognac

1 part Kirschwasser

Garnish: chocolate powder

Shake with ice and strain into a cocktail glass. Shake
chocolate powder on top.

EMBRACE

2 parts gin

1 part triple sec

Splash of grape juice

Stir with ice and strain into a cocktail glass.

EMOTIONAL

2 parts orange juice
1 part vodka
1 part Parfait Amour
1 part triple sec
1 part tonic water
Build on ice in a highball glass and stir.

EMPEROR'S VINE

1 part gin
1 part Mandarine Napoléon®
1 part grape juice
Stir with ice and strain into a cocktail glass.

EMPIRE

3 parts gin
2 parts apricot brandy
1 part apple brandy
Splash of orange juice
Stir with ice and strain into a cocktail glass.

EROTICA

4 parts sparkling wine

1 part gin

Splash of lemon juice

Pinch of sugar

Garnish: cherry and orange slice

Pour into a tall glass half filled with ice. Garnish with cherry and orange slice.

ESCAPE

1 part gin

Splash of Bols® Coconut

Splash of créme de banana

Stir with ice and strain into a cocktail glass.

ESPECIALLY ROUGH

2 parts lemon-lime soda

1 part apple brandy

1 part anisette

Shake with ice and strain into a cocktail glass.

ESPRESSO MARTINI

1 part vodka
1 part Kahlua®
1 part espresso
Garnish: whipped cream
Shake with ice and strain into a cocktail glass. Garnish
with whipped cream.

ESSENCE

2 parts bourbon
1 part crème de banana
1 part cherry brandy
Splash of grapefruit juice
Shake with ice and strain into a cocktail glass.

ETHIOPIAN CAMEL BASHER

1 part vodka
1 part orange juice
1 part Kirschwasser
Shake with ice and strain into a cocktail glass.

EVERYTHING COUNTS

2 parts tomato juice
1 part tequila
1 part Amaretto
Splash of whiskey
Splash of hot sauce
Build on ice in a highball glass.

EXOTIC TULIP

1 part cachaça
1 part sweet vermouth
Splash of apricot brandy
Shake with ice and strain into a cocktail glass.

FASTER FASTER

1 part light rum
1 part crème de banana
1 part blackberry brandy
Splash of grenadine
Splash of sour mix
Shake with ice and strain into a cocktail glass.

FEELS LIKE SUMMER

2 parts orange juice
1 part gin
1 part Mandarine Napoléon®
Splash of grenadine
Stir with ice and strain into a cocktail glass.

FIELDS OF CREAM

2 parts Amaretto
1 part peach schnapps
1 part strawberry liqueur
1 part cream
Shake with ice and strain into a cocktail glass.

FIERCE PASSION

2 parts Passoã®
1 part white grape juice
1 part tonic water
Garnish: pineapple wedge
Shake with ice and strain into a cocktail glass. Garnish
with pineapple wedge.

FIFI MARTINI

2 parts brandy
1 part dry vermouth
Splash of grenadine
Shake with ice and strain into a cocktail glass.

FINK

1 part Bacardi® Limon
1 part apple cider
Shake with ice and strain into a cocktail glass.

FIERY LATIN

3 parts light rum
1 part coffee brandy
1 part cream
Splash of Bacardi® 151
Shake light rum, coffee brandy, and cream
with ice and strain into a cocktail glass.
Top with Bacardi® 151.

FIRST THING

2 parts dark rum
1 part coffee liqueur
1 part cola
Garnish: scoop of vanilla ice cream
Build on ice in a highball glass and stir.
Top with scoop of vanilla ice cream.

FLUFF COCKTAIL

2 parts cream
1 part chocolate vodka
1 part Bailey's Irish Cream®
1 part white crème de cacao
Splash of peanut liqueur
Shake with ice and strain into a cocktail glass.

FRANCOPHILE

1 part brandy
1 part Grand Marnier®
1 part Lillet
Splash of lemon juice
Shake with ice and strain into a cocktail glass.

FRANCO DE ANIMALIA

2 parts vodka

1 part spiced rum

1 part Amaretto

1 part mango juice

1 part lemon juice (freshly squeezed)

Splash of hot sauce

Garnish: maraschino cherry and frog leg
sword spear

Shake with ice and strain into a double rocks glass.
Garnish with maraschino cherry and frog leg sword spear.

FRANKLY SPEAKING

2 parts sparkling wine

1 part Cognac

Splash of pastis

Pour into a wine glass and stir.

FRESHEN UP

1 part vodka
1 part Midori®
1 part lemonade
Splash of Chambord®
Shake with ice and strain into a rocks glass.

FRIENDSHIP

3 parts lemonade
1 part Bols® Lychee
1 part Absolut® Citron
Splash of sloe gin
Splash of lime juice (freshly squeezed)
Build on ice in a tall glass and stir.

FROG IN A STRAWBERRY FIELD

3 parts tequila
1 part sloe gin
1 part sweet vermouth
Garnish: strawberry
Shake with ice and strain into a cocktail glass. Garnish
with strawberry.

FROTHY REDHEAD

1 part red wine
1 part cola
1 scoop of vanilla ice cream
Pinch of sugar
Mix in a blender and pour into a wine glass.

FROU FROU

1 part advocaat
1 part lemonade
Shake with ice and strain into a cocktail glass.

FRUIT ORGY

1 part vodka
1 part mango schnapps
1 part crème de banana
1 part pineapple juice
Shake with ice and strain into a cocktail glass.

FRUIT SALAD

1 part vodka
1 part peach schnapps
1 part pineapple juice
1 part cranberry juice
Garnish: cherry
Shake with ice and strain into a cocktail glass. Garnish
with cherry.

FRUIT TINGLE

2 parts lemonade
1 part blue curaçao
1 part raspberry liqueur
Shake with ice and strain into a cocktail glass.

FRUITOPIA

1 part Amaretto
1 part Malibu Coconut Rum®
1 part pineapple juice
1 part apple juice
Shake with ice and strain into a cocktail glass.

FRUITY LOOPS

1 part orange juice
1 part apple schnapps
Build on ice in a highball glass and stir.

FRUITY MARTINI

1 part gin
1 part grapefruit juice
1 part lemonade
Splash of dry vermouth
Stir with ice and strain into a cocktail glass.

FUCK ME

1 part light rum
1 part coconut brandy
1 part pineapple juice
Shake with ice and strain into a cocktail glass.

FUCKING HOT

2 parts pineapple juice
1 part light rum
1 part blue curaçao
1 part coconut cream
Build on ice in a highball glass and stir.

FULL MONTY

3 parts orange juice
1 part vodka
1 part Pisang Ambon®
1 part Passoã®
Garnish: lemon wedge
Build on ice in a tall glass and stir.
Garnish with lemon wedge.

FULL NELSON

1 part crème de banana
1 part green crème de menthe
1 part cream
Shake with ice and strain into a cocktail glass.

FUNKY FIX

1 part white wine
1 part cola
1 part soda
Splash of lime juice
Pour into a wine glass.

FUNNEL CLOUD

2 parts ginger ale
1 part Southern Comfort®
Shake with ice and strain into a rocks glass.

FUZZY NAVEL

2 parts orange juice
1 part peach schnapps
Build on ice in a highball glass.

GALACTIC GARGLE BLASTER

1 part Tia Maria®
1 part cherry brandy
1 part apple cider
Splash of lime juice
Splash of soda water
Build on ice in a highball glass and stir.

GALACTIC JUICE

2 parts sparkling wine
Splash of orange vodka
Splash of blue curaçao
Pinch of sugar
Dash of bitters
Pour into a champagne flute.

GALAXY

2 parts cream
1 part Bailey's Irish Cream®
1 part blue curaçao
1 part Chambord®
Shake with ice and strain into a cocktail glass.

GALAXY OF VANILLA

2 parts Tuaca®
2 parts pineapple juice
1 part cream
Build on ice in a highball glass and stir.

GATES OF HELL

1 part tequila
Splash of lemon juice
Splash of lime juice
Splash of cherry brandy
Garnish: lime twist

Shake tequila, lemon juice, and lime juice with ice and strain into a cocktail glass. Float cherry brandy on top. Garnish with lime twist.

GAYLEY AVENUE MARGARITA

2 parts Jose Cuervo® tequila
2 parts strawberry liqueur
2 parts sour mix
1 part triple sec
Garnish: cherry

Mix with ice in a blender. Pour into a cocktail glass. Garnish with cherry.

GEEZ LOUISE

3 parts passion fruit juice
1 part Amaretto
1 part sweet vermouth
Splash of grenadine
Build on ice in a highball glass and stir.

GEM

2 parts rum
1 part crème de banana
1 part lemon juice
Garnish: cherry
Shake with ice and strain into a cocktail glass. Garnish
with cherry.

GENEVA CONVENTION

4 parts vodka
1 part Goldschläger®
1 part Everclear®
Shake with ice and strain into a cocktail glass.

GEORGIA GIN

3 parts gin
2 parts orange juice
1 part Southern Comfort®
Splash of peach schnapps
Stir with ice and strain into a cocktail glass.

GEORGIA JULEP

1 part Cognac
1 part peach brandy
Shake with ice and strain into a cocktail glass.

GEORGIA SODA

2 parts peach vodka
1 part soda
1 part pineapple juice
Shake with ice and strain into a cocktail glass.

GERMAN CHOCOLATE CAKE

1 part Malibu Coconut Rum®

1 part brown crème de cacao

1 part cream

Splash of Frangelico®

Shake with ice and strain into a cocktail glass.

GET OVER IT

2 parts brandy

1 part blackberry schnapps

1 part sherry

Dash of bitters

Shake with ice and strain into a cocktail glass.

GET PAID

2 parts Cognac
1 part crème de banana
1 part triple sec
Splash of grenadine
Garnish: Cherry

Shake with ice and strain into a cocktail glass. Garnish with cherry.

GET RANDY

2 parts cranberry juice
1 part gin
1 part vodka
1 part triple sec
Splash of lemon-lime soda
Garnish: lime twist

Build on ice in a highball glass.
Garnish with lime twist.

GG

2 parts ginger ale
1 part Galliano®
Shake with ice and strain into a rocks glass.

GHOSTBUSTER

3 parts vanilla milk
1 part vodka
1 part Bailey's Irish Cream®
1 part Kahlua®
Build on ice in a highball glass and stir.

GIBSON

1 part gin
Dash of dry vermouth
Garnish: 3 cocktail onions
Stir with ice and strain into a cocktail glass. Garnish
with cocktail onions.

GIDDY UP

2 parts peach schnapps
2 parts vodka
1 part apple cider
Shake with ice and strain into a cocktail glass.

GIMLET

1 part vodka
Splash of lime juice
Garnish: lime wedge
Build on ice in a rocks glass.
Garnish with lime wedge.

GIMME MORE

3 parts cream
1 part melon liqueur
1 part tequila
1 part banana liqueur
Garnish: orange twist
Shake with ice and strain into a cocktail glass. Garnish
with orange twist.

GIN ALOHA

1 part gin
1 part triple sec
Splash of pineapple juice
Dash of bitters
Stir with ice and strain into a cocktail glass.

GIN AND BEAR IT

3 parts gin
1 part Galliano®
Splash of orange juice
Garnish: orange slice
Stir with ice and strain into a cocktail glass. Garnish
with orange slice.

GIN HORNET

3 parts gin
1 part sherry
1 part scotch
Stir with ice and strain into a cocktail glass.

GIN RICKEY

2 parts soda
1 part gin
Garnish: lime wedge
Build on ice in a highball glass.
Garnish with lime wedge.

GIN-CHERRY BOMB

2 parts gin
1 part Cointreau®
1 part lime juice (freshly squeezed)
1 part cherry schnapps
Splash of tonic water
Dash of bitters
Stir with ice and strain into a cocktail glass.

GINELICO

1 part gin
Splash of Frangelico®
Garnish: ground nutmeg
Stir with ice and strain into a cocktail glass. Garnish
with ground nutmeg.

GINGER PEACH

2 parts gin
1 part peach schnapps
1 part triple sec
Splash of orange juice
Stir with ice and strain into a cocktail glass.

GINGER SNAP

3 parts Bols® Genever
1 part melon liqueur
Splash of lime juice (freshly squeezed)
Shake with ice and strain into a cocktail glass.

GINGER SODA

2 parts vodka
1 part ginger liqueur
1 part soda
Splash of lime juice
Shake with ice and strain into a cocktail glass.

GINGER SPICE

2 parts gin
1 part peppermint schnapps
1 part lemon-lime soda
Pinch of sugar
Garnish: mint sprig and lemon wedge
Build on ice in a highball glass. Garnish with mint sprig
and lemon wedge.

GINGY BANANA

1 part Tanqueray®
1 part crème de banana
Splash of lime juice (freshly squeezed)
Stir with ice and strain into a cocktail glass.

GIVE ME A DIME

1 part white crème de cacao
1 part butterscotch schnapps
Shake with ice and strain into a cocktail glass.

GLACIER

1 part light rum
1 part blackberry schnapps
1 part white crème de cacao
1 part cold coffee
Shake with ice and strain into a cocktail glass.

GLORY

2 parts brandy
2 parts Campari®
1 parts scotch
1 part Amaretto
Dash of dry vermouth
Shake with ice and strain into a cocktail glass.

GODCHILD

3 parts brandy
1 part Amaretto
Build on ice in a rocks glass.

GODFATHER

3 parts scotch
1 part Amaretto
Build on ice in a rocks glass.

GODMOTHER

3 parts vodka
1 part Amaretto
Build on ice in a rocks glass.

GOING STEADY

1 part Kahlua®
1 part Malibu Coconut Rum®
1 part crème de noyaux
1 part cream
Shake with ice and strain into a cocktail glass.

GOLDEN BANANA

1 part Goldschläger®
1 part coffee liqueur
1 part crème de banana
1 part cream
Shake with ice and strain into a cocktail glass.

GOLDEN CADILLAC

2 parts cream
1 part white crème de cacao
1 part Galliano®
Shake with ice and strain into a cocktail glass.

GOLDEN DAZE

3 parts gin
2 parts orange juice
1 part peach brandy
Stir with ice and strain into a cocktail glass.

GOLDEN DREAM

2 parts Galliano®
1 part triple sec
Splash of orange juice
Splash of cream
Shake with ice and strain into a cocktail glass.

GOLDEN GATE

2 parts brandy
1 part blue curaçao
1 part light rum
Garnish: cherry
Shake with ice and strain into a cocktail glass. Garnish
with cherry.

GOLFER

1 part vodka
1 part gin
Dash of dry vermouth
Garnish: lemon twist
Stir with ice and strain into a cocktail glass. Garnish
with lemon twist.

GOOD MORNING MEXICO

2 parts Kahlua®
1 part Jose Cuervo® tequila
Splash of lime juice
Shake with ice and strain into a cocktail glass.

GOOD MORNING WORLD

2 parts Kahlua®
1 part dark rum
Splash of lime juice
Shake with ice and strain into a cocktail glass.

GOODNIGHT KISS

3 parts champagne
1 part Campari®
Pinch of sugar
Dash of bitters

Drop sugar and bitters into a champagne flute. Pour champagne and add Campari®.

GOODY TWO SHOES

1 part dark rum
1 part peach schnapps
1 part coconut liqueur
1 part pineapple juice
1 part orange juice
Garnish: pineapple wedge

Shake with ice and strain into a cocktail glass. Garnish with pineapple wedge.

GOOP

2 parts lemonade
1 part advocaat
1 part peach schnapps
Splash of anisette
Build on ice in a highball glass and stir.

GRAND OCCASION

1 part light rum
Splash of white crème de cacao
Splash of Grand Marnier®
Shake with ice and strain into a cocktail glass.

GRAND RIO

2 parts cachaça
1 part Grand Marnier®
1 part lemonade
Garnish: basil leaves
Shake with ice and strain into a cocktail glass. Garnish
with basil leaves.

GRAND SODA

2 parts Aperol
1 part Grand Marnier®
1 part soda
Shake with ice and strain into a cocktail glass.

GRANDDADDY

2 parts apple brandy
1 part Cognac
1 part Grand Marnier®
Shake with ice and strain into a cocktail glass.

GRAPE APE

1 part vodka
1 part grape juice
Splash of crème de banana
Shake with ice and strain into a cocktail glass.

GRAPE SODA

2 parts lemon–lime soda
1 part grape vodka
Shake with ice and strain into a cocktail glass.

GRAPEFRUIT COCKTAIL

1 part gin
1 part grapefruit juice
Garnish: maraschino cherry
Stir with ice and strain into a cocktail glass. Garnish
with maraschino cherry.

GRAPEFRUIT NOG

2 parts grapefruit juice
1 part brandy
1 part crème de banana
1 egg white
Shake with ice and strain into a cocktail glass.

GRAPESCHLÄGER

3 parts grape soda
1 part Goldschläger®
Build on ice in a highball glass and stir.

GRAPEVINE COCKTAIL

2 parts white wine
1 part grape soda
Pour into a wine glass and stir.

GRAPPA LEMONADE

1 part grappa
1 part lemonade
Shake with ice and strain into a cocktail glass.

GRAPPATINI

1 part grappa
Dash of dry vermouth
Shake with ice and strain into a cocktail glass.

GRASSHOPPER

2 parts cream
1 part white crème de cacao
1 part green crème de menthe
Shake with ice and strain into a cocktail glass.

GREASED LIGHTNING

1 part gin
Dash of cherry brandy
Dash of dry vermouth
Shake with ice and strain into a cocktail glass.

GREEN ALEXANDER

2 parts gin
2 parts cream
1 part green crème de menthe
Garnish: ground nutmeg
Shake with ice and strain into a cocktail glass. Garnish
with ground nutmeg.

GREEN MIRAGE

2 parts vodka
1 part Galliano®
Dash of dry vermouth
Dash of blue curaçao
Shake with ice and strain into a cocktail glass.

GREEN RUSSIAN

1 part vodka
1 part Midori®
1 tablespoon caramel syrup
Shake with ice and strain into a cocktail glass.

GRENATINI

1 part vodka
Splash of Amaretto
Splash of grenadine
Garnish: cherry
Shake with ice and strain into a cocktail glass. Garnish
with cherry.

GRETA GARBO

1 part Bacardi® light rum
Splash of Bols® Maraschino
Splash of lime juice (freshly squeezed)
Splash of pastis
Pinch of sugar
Shake with ice and strain into a cocktail glass.

GREYHOUND

2 parts grapefruit juice
1 part vodka
Build on ice in a highball glass.

GRINGO

2 parts vanilla vodka
1 part crème de banana
1 part banana juice
1 part coconut milk
Shake with ice and strain into a cocktail glass.

GUAVA COOLER

2 parts soda
2 parts light rum
1 part guava juice
Build on ice in a highball glass and stir.

GUAVABERRY BREEZE

1 part vodka
1 part guavaberry liqueur
1 part cranberry juice
Shake with ice and strain into a cocktail glass.

GUAVABERRY ROYALE

2 parts sparkling wine
1 part guava juice
Pour into a champagne flute and stir.

GUAVALADA

3 parts coconut rum
1 part guava juice
1 part coconut milk
Garnish: pineapple wedge and cherry
Shake with ice and strain into a cocktail glass. Garnish with pineapple wedge and cherry.

GUAVAMANIA

2 parts light rum
1 part guava juice
Splash of triple sec
Shake with ice and strain into a cocktail glass.

HAIR RAISER

1 part vodka

Splash of whiskey

Shake with ice and strain into a cocktail glass.

HAIRY NAVEL

2 parts orange juice

1 part vodka

1 part peach schnapps

Build on ice in a highball glass.

HAMMERHEAD

1 part Amaretto
1 part blue curaçao
1 part amber rum
Splash of Southern Comfort®
Shake with ice and strain into a cocktail glass.

HANKHATTAN

1 part Bulleit Bourbon®
Splash of sweet vermouth
Stir with ice and strain into a cocktail glass.

HAPPY LANDINGS

2 parts sloe gin
1 part scotch
Splash of grenadine
Shake with ice and strain into a cocktail glass.

HAREM DREAM

2 parts currant vodka
1 part raspberry liqueur
1 part cranberry juice
Garnish: lime wedge
Shake with ice and strain into a cocktail glass.

HARLEM MUGGER

1 part sparkling wine
Splash of vodka
Splash of gin
Splash of light rum
Splash of tequila
Splash of cranberry juice
Garnish: lime wedge
Build over ice in tall glass. Garnish with lime wedge.

HARVEY WALLBANGER

2 parts orange juice
1 part vodka
Splash of Galliano®
Pour vodka and orange juice in a highball glass and stir.
Top with Galliano®.

HAT TRICK

1 part dark rum
1 part light rum
1 part sweet vermouth
Shake with ice and strain into a cocktail glass.

HAVANA COCKTAIL

2 parts pineapple juice
1 part light rum
Splash of lemon juice
Shake with ice and strain into a cocktail glass.

HAWAIIAN MARTINI

4 parts gin
1 part blue curaçao
Splash of pineapple juice
Splash of grenadine
Stir with ice and strain into a cocktail glass.

HAWAIIAN MEXICAN

1 part tequila
1 part pineapple juice
Splash of grenadine
Shake with ice and strain into a cocktail glass.

HAZEL'S NUT

2 parts Pisang Ambon®
2 parts Frangelico®
1 part grapefruit juice
Shake with ice and strain into a cocktail glass.

HAZELNUT MARTINI

3 parts vodka
1 part Frangelico®
Shake with ice and strain into a cocktail glass.

HEARTS AFIRE

2 parts apricot brandy
1 part cranberry juice
1 part soda
Garnish: lemon twist
Shake with ice and strain into a cocktail glass. Garnish
with lemon twist.

HER NAME IN LIGHTS

2 parts vodka
1 part Chartreuse®
Splash of Galliano®
Splash of blue curaçao
Splash of lemon juice
Garnish: maraschino cherry
Shake with ice and strain into a cocktail glass. Garnish with cherry.

HIGH FASHION

1 part vodka
Splash of scotch
Splash of blue curaçao
Garnish: orange twist
Shake with ice and strain into a cocktail glass. Garnish with orange twist.

HIGH IMPACT

1 part apricot brandy
1 part bourbon
Splash of lime juice (freshly squeezed)
Dash of dry vermouth
Shake with ice and strain into a cocktail glass.

HIGHBALL

2 parts ginger ale
1 part whiskey
Build on ice in a highball glass.

HIJACK

2 parts white wine
1 part brandy
1 sugar cube
Garnish: orange slice
Shake and strain into a rocks glass filled with ice.
Garnish with orange slice.

HIPPITY DIPPITY

2 parts orange juice
1 part spiced rum
Splash of triple sec
Splash of lime juice
Splash of grenadine
Garnish: cherry

Build on ice in highball glass and stir. Garnish with cherry.

HIT THE DECK

2 parts vodka
1 part crème de banana
1 part Campari®
Splash of grenadine
Splash of lime juice
Garnish: cherry

Shake with ice and strain into a cocktail glass. Garnish with cherry.

HITCHCOCKTAIL

1 part pineapple juice

1 part orange juice

1 part dry vermouth

Build on ice in a highball glass and stir.

HOMECOMING

1 part gin

1 part apricot brandy

Splash of lemon juice

Dash of dry vermouth

Garnish: maraschino cherry

Stir with ice and strain into a cocktail glass. Garnish
with maraschino cherry.

HONEYDEW MARTINI

4 parts vodka
1 part blue curaçao
1 part melon liqueur
Garnish: lemon twist

Shake with ice and strain into a cocktail glass. Garnish
with lemon twist.

HONEYMOON COCKTAIL

1 part apple brandy
1 part Bénédictine
Splash of triple sec
Splash of lemon juice (freshly squeezed)

Shake with ice and strain into a cocktail glass.

HONEYMOON IN HAWAII

1 part cherry vodka
1 part maraschino liqueur
1 part pineapple juice
1 part coconut cream

Shake with ice and strain into a cocktail glass.

HONOLULU COCKTAIL

2 parts vodka

1 part crème de cassis

1 part pineapple juice

1 part banana juice

Shake with ice and strain into a cocktail glass.

HONOLULU HAMMER

3 parts vodka

1 part Amaretto

Splash of pineapple juice

Splash of grenadine

Shake with ice and strain into a cocktail glass.

HOOT MON

1 part scotch

Dash of Bénédictine

Dash of sweet vermouth

Shake with ice and strain into a cocktail glass.

HOPEFUL

2 parts gin
1 part crème de banana
1 part strawberry liqueur
Splash of pineapple juice
Stir with ice and strain into a cocktail glass.

HORNY BASTARD

1 part gin
1 part apple brandy
Splash of anisette
Dash of grenadine
Stir with ice and strain into a cocktail glass.

HOT COCOA DESERT

2 parts hot cocoa
2 parts chocolate liqueur
1 part crème de noyaux
1 part cherry brandy
Pour into an Irish coffee glass and stir.

HOT TODDY

1 part whiskey

1 part hot water

Garnish: lemon twist

Pour into an Irish coffee glass. Garnish with lemon
twist.

HUNTING PINK

2 parts tequila

2 parts strawberry liqueur

1 part sambuca

1 egg white

Shake with ice and strain into a cocktail glass.

HURRICANE

3 parts sour mix

1 part light rum

1 part dark rum

1 part grenadine

Splash of cranberry juice

Splash of pineapple juice

Splash of Bacardi 151®

Garnish: orange slice and cherry

Build on ice in a tall glass and stir. Top with Bacardi 151®. Garnish with orange slice and cherry.

HUSTLER'S BREAKFAST

2 parts bourbon

2 parts sour mix

1 part white crème de cacao

Dash of grenadine

Dash of bitters

Shake with ice and strain into a cocktail glass.

I LOVE YOU

2 parts Bacardi Gold Reserve®
2 parts apricot brandy
1 part peach schnapps
Splash of Amaretto
Splash of orange juice
Garnish: mint sprig

Shake with ice and strain into a cocktail glass. Garnish
with mint sprig.

I WANT YOU

1 part white créme de cacao
1 part apricot brandy
1 part cream
Splash of soda
Shake with ice and strain into a cocktail glass.

ICEBERG IN RADIOACTIVE WATER

3 parts Midori®
3 parts pineapple juice
1 part Malibu Coconut Rum®
1 part banana liqueur
Garnish: scoop of vanilla ice cream
Build on ice in a tall glass and stir.
Top with scoop of vanilla ice cream.

IGUANA

3 parts sour mix
2 parts vanilla vodka
1 part tequila
Garnish: lime wedge
Shake with ice and strain into a cocktail glass. Garnish
with lime wedge.

ILLUSION

2 parts Malibu Coconut Rum®
1 part Midori®
1 part Grey Goose® vodka
1 part Cointreau®
Splash of pineapple juice
Shake with ice and strain into a cocktail glass.

IN COLD BLOOD

2 parts bourbon
1 part peppermint schnapps
1 part grenadine
Dash of bitters
Pinch of sugar
Splash of soda
Garnish: cherry

Build on ice in a tall glass and stir. Garnish with cherry.

IN MINT CONDITION

1 part peppermint schnapps
1 part blue curaçao
1 part apricot brandy
1 part lemon–lime soda

Shake with ice and strain into a cocktail glass.

IN VAIN

2 parts sherry

1 part chocolate liqueur

1 part Cognac

1 egg yolk

Pinch of sugar

Shake with ice and strain into a cocktail glass.

INCA FIRE

1 part vodka

1 part pisco

1 part grenadine

Shake with ice and strain into a cocktail glass.

INSPIRATIONAL

2 parts Cognac

1 part light rum

Splash of lime juice

Shake with ice and strain into a cocktail glass.

INTRIGUE COCKTAIL

1 part Kahlua®
1 part crème de banana
Splash of sweet vermouth
Shake with ice and strain into a cocktail glass.

IRISH CHEER

1 part whiskey
Splash of melon liqueur
Splash of sweet vermouth
Shake and strain into a rocks glass filled with ice.

IRISH COFFEE

2 parts coffee
1 part Irish whiskey
Garnish: whipped cream
Pour into an Irish coffee glass.
Top with whipped cream.

IRISH COLONEL

1 part bourbon
1 part Bailey's Irish Cream®
1 part cherry cola
Shake with ice and strain into a rocks glass.

IRISH CREAM FREEZE

1 part Bailey's Irish Cream®
1 part cream
2 scoops of vanilla ice cream
Mix with ice in a blender and pour into a highball glass.

IRISH GINGY

1 part Bailey's Irish Cream®
1 part ginger liqueur
1 part ginger ale
Splash of sweet vermouth
Shake with ice and strain into a cocktail glass.

IRISH HONEY

1 part whiskey
1 part cream
1 tablespoon of honey
Shake with ice and strain into a cocktail glass.

ISLAND OF SANTA LUCIA

1 part Kahlua®
1 part spiced rum
Shake with ice and strain into a rocks glass filled with ice.

IT'S A MYSTERY

1 part gin
Splash of single malt scotch
Garnish: olive
Stir with ice and strain into a cocktail glass. Garnish with olive.

IT'S MIDNIGHT

2 parts apricot brandy
1 part black sambuca
Splash of lemon juice
Shake with ice and strain into a cocktail glass.

IT'S THE DRINK TALKING

1 part whiskey
Splash of Amaretto
Splash of crème de banana
Splash of grenadine
Garnish: cherry
Shake with ice and strain into a cocktail glass. Garnish with cherry.

ITALIAN CREAMSICLE

1 part Amaretto
1 part triple sec
1 part cream
Shake with ice and strain into a cocktail glass.

ITALIAN DELIGHT

2 parts cream

1 part Amaretto

Splash of orange juice

Garnish: cherry

Shake with ice and strain into a cocktail glass. Garnish with cherry.

ITALIAN STALLION

2 parts bourbon

1 part Campari®

Dash of sweet vermouth

Garnish: lemon twist

Shake with ice and strain into a cocktail glass. Garnish with lemon twist.

JACK OF ALL TRADES

2 parts vodka
1 part brandy
1 part crème de cassis
1 part triple sec
Dash of bitters
Shake with ice and strain into a cocktail glass.

JACK'S BANANA

2 parts applejack
1 part vodka
1 part crème de banana
1 egg white
Shake with ice and strain into a cocktail glass.

JACUZZI

3 parts champagne

1 part gin

Splash of orange juice

Splash of passion fruit juice

Pour champagne into a champagne flute. Swirl gin, orange juice, and passion fruit juice with ice and strain over the champagne.

JADE

2 parts light rum

1 part green crème de menthe

1 part triple sec

Splash of lime juice

Pinch of sugar

Garnish: lime wedge

Shake with ice and strain into a cocktail glass. Garnish with lime wedge.

JÄGERMONSTER

1 part Jägermeister®
1 part grenadine
1 part orange juice
Shake with ice and strain into a rocks glass.

JAMAICAN ME CRAZY

1 part Bacardi® light rum
1 part Malibu Coconut Rum®
1 part banana liqueur
Splash of cranberry juice
Splash of pineapple juice
Shake with ice and strain into a rocks glass.

JAMAICAN SUNRISE

1 part mango vodka
1 part peach schnapps
Splash of orange juice
Splash of cranberry juice
Shake with ice and strain into a cocktail glass.

JAMES BOND MARTINI

3 parts gin
1 part vodka
Splash of Lillet
Garnish: lemon peel

Shake with ice and strain into a goblet. Garnish with lemon peel. The gin will be bruised, but James Bond famously likes his martinis "shaken, not stirred."

JAPANESE SLIPPER

1 part Midori®
1 part Cointreau®
Splash of lime juice

Shake with ice and strain into a cocktail glass.

JELLY BEAN

2 parts anisette
1 part blackberry brandy
1 part Southern Comfort®

Build on ice in a rocks glass.

JERSEY LIGHTNING

1 part apple brandy

Splash of sweet vermouth

Splash of lime juice

Shake with ice and strain into a cocktail glass.

JET BLACK

1 part gin

Splash of sweet vermouth

Splash of black sambuca

Stir with ice and strain into a cocktail glass.

JIBBER JABBER

1 part Malibu Coconut Rum®

1 part crème de banana

1 part strawberry liqueur

1 part orange juice

Shake with ice and strain into a cocktail glass.

JOHN COLLINS

3 parts sour mix
2 parts whiskey
1 part soda
Garnish: orange slice and cherry
Build on ice in a tall glass and stir. Garnish with orange slice and cherry.

JOLLY ROGER

1 part dark rum
1 part banana liqueur
Splash of lemon juice
Shake with ice and strain into a rocks glass filled with ice.

JONESY

2 parts dark rum
1 part brown crème de cacao
Shake with ice and strain into a rocks glass filled with ice.

JORDIELIGHT

2 parts vodka
1 part crème de cassis
1 part pineapple juice
1 part cranberry juice
Garnish: lime wedge

Shake with ice and strain into a cocktail glass. Garnish with lime wedge.

JOSE'S VOICE

2 parts orange juice
1 part tequila
1 part crème de cassis
1 part melon liqueur
Garnish: lime slice

Shake with ice and strain into a cocktail glass. Garnish with lime slice.

JUPITER

2 parts gin

1 part crème de violette

Splash of orange juice

Dash of dry vermouth

Stir with ice and strain into a cocktail glass.

JUST A GIGOLO

2 parts Bacardi® light rum

1 part cherry brandy

1 part pineapple juice

Garnish: pineapple wedge

Shake with ice and strain into a cocktail glass. Garnish with pineapple wedge.

JUST ENJOY IT

1 part whiskey

1 part blackberry schnapps

Splash of lime juice

Shake with ice and strain into a cocktail glass.

JUST NOT RIGHT

4 parts vodka

1 part peppermint schnapps

Shake with ice and strain into a cocktail glass.

KAMIKAZE

3 parts vodka
1 part triple sec
Splash of lime juice
Garnish: lime wedge
Build on ice in a rocks glass. Garnish with lime wedge.

KEEP 'EM COMING

1 part gin
1 part Kirschwasser
Splash of lime juice
Dash of dry vermouth
Stir with ice and strain into a cocktail glass.

KEEP IT CLEAN

2 parts chocolate milk
1 part Canadian Club® whiskey
1 part Bailey's Irish Cream®
1 part Kahlua®
Shake with ice and strain into a cocktail glass.

KEEP IT LIGHT

2 parts cola
1 part root beer vodka
Build on ice in a highball glass.

KEEP ON CRACKIN'

2 parts scotch
1 part cranberry juice
1 part soda
Garnish: lime wedge
Shake with ice and strain into a cocktail glass. Garnish
with lime wedge.

KEEP QUIET

2 parts scotch
1 part Aperol
1 part sweet vermouth
Shake with ice and strain into a cocktail glass.

KEEP SMILING

3 part light rum
1 part pineapple juice
Splash of maraschino liqueur
Garnish: cherry
Shake with ice and strain into a cocktail glass. Garnish
with cherry.

KENTUCKY KISS

1 part bourbon
1 part Southern Comfort®
Garnish: cherry
Shake with ice and strain into a rocks glass filled with
ice. Garnish with cherry.

KEOKE COFFEE

2 parts coffee

1 part brown crème de cacao

1 part Kahlua®

1 part brandy

Garnish: whipped cream

Pour into an Irish coffee glass. Top with whipped cream.

KEY LIME PIE

1 part Licor 43®

1 part cream

1 part lime juice

Shake with ice and strain into a cocktail glass.

KICK BACK

2 parts raspberry liqueur

1 part pineapple juice

1 part cream

Shake with ice and strain into a cocktail glass.

KICK IN THE PANTS

1 part Cognac

1 part bourbon

1 part blue curaçao

Garnish: lemon slice

Shake with ice and strain into a cocktail glass. Garnish
with lemon slice.

KILLER PUNCH

1 part Southern Comfort®

1 part Midori®

Splash of crème de noyaux

Splash of cranberry juice

Shake with ice and strain into a cocktail glass.

KINKY ORGASM

3 parts cranberry juice
1 part banana vodka
1 part peach schnapps
1 part raspberry liqueur
Splash of orange juice
Build on ice in a highball glass and stir.

KIR

3 parts white wine
1 part crème de cassis
Garnish: lemon twist
Pour into a wine glass. Garnish with lemon twist.

KIR ROYALE

3 parts champagne
1 part Chambord®
Garnish: lemon twist
Pour into a champagne flute. Garnish with lemon twist.

KISS MY MONKEY

1 part vanilla vodka

1 part banana liqueur

1 part cream

1 part advocaat

Shake with ice and strain into a cocktail glass.

KIWI SPARKLER

2 parts sparkling wine

1 part kiwi liqueur

Pour into a wine glass and stir.

KNICKERBOCKER KNOCKER

1 part melon liqueur

1 part peach schnapps

1 part crème de banana

1 part orange juice

1 part cranberry juice

1 part pineapple juice

Build on ice in a tall glass and stir.

KNOCK OUT

1 part brandy
1 part sloe gin
1 tablespoon syrup
Shake with ice and strain into a cocktail glass.

KNOCKOUT PUNCH

2 parts fruit punch
1 part sloe gin
1 part Bols® Blue
Garnish: blueberries
Build on ice in a highball glass and stir. Garnish with blueberries.

LA BOMBA

2 parts tequila
1 part triple sec
Splash of pineapple juice
Splash of orange juice
Splash of grenadine
Shake with ice and strain into a cocktail glass.

LA JOLLA

2 parts brandy
1 part crème de banana
Splash of lemon juice
Splash of orange juice
Shake with ice and strain into a cocktail glass.

LA VIDA LOCA

1 part Malibu Coconut Rum®

1 part crème de banana

1 part cherry brandy

1 part melon liqueur

Shake with ice and strain into a cocktail glass.

LADIES COCKTAIL

2 parts whiskey

1 part anisette

Dash of bitters

Shake with ice and strain into a cocktail glass.

LADY FINGER

2 parts gin

2 parts cherry brandy

2 parts orange juice

1 part Kirschwasser

Stir with ice and strain into a cocktail glass.

LADY KILLER

2 parts gin
1 part cream
1 egg white
Splash of grenadine
Stir with ice and strain into a cocktail glass.

LADY LIBERTY IN A THONG

3 parts dark rum
1 part coffee brandy
Splash of lemon juice
Shake with ice and strain into a cocktail glass.

LAMB BROTHERS

3 parts pineapple juice
2 parts dark rum
1 part crème de cassis
Build on ice in a highball glass and stir.

LANDED GENTRY

3 parts dark rum
1 part Tia Maria®
1 part cream
Shake with ice and strain into a cocktail glass.

LAUGHING AT THE WAVES

2 parts vodka
1 part Campari®
Dash of dry vermouth
Garnish: lemon twist
Shake with ice and strain into a cocktail glass. Garnish
with lemon twist.

LEAP YEAR

2 parts gin
1 part Grand Marnier®
Splash of sweet vermouth
Splash of lemon juice
Stir with ice and strain into a cocktail glass.

LEAVE QUIETLY

2 parts Lillet
1 part gin
1 part Parfait Amour
Dash of bitters
Stir with ice and strain into a cocktail glass.

LEMON CAKE

1 part light rum
1 part Bailey's Irish Cream®
1 part lemon juice
1 scoop of vanilla ice cream
Garnish: whipped cream
Mix in a blender and pour into a highball glass. Garnish with whipped cream.

LEMON CUP

3 parts Pimm's® No. 1
2 parts lemonade
1 part grenadine
Shake with ice and strain into a cocktail glass.

LEMON SPRITZER

2 parts sparkling wine
1 part iced tea
1 part lemon schnapps
Garnish: lemon wedge

Pour into a wine glass and stir. Garnish with lemon wedge.

LEMON-PEACH PUNCH

1 part limoncello
Splash of peach schnapps

Shake with ice and strain into a cocktail glass.

LEPRECHAUN DELIGHT

2 parts cream
1 part green crème de menthe
1 part chocolate liqueur
1 part crème de banana
Garnish: scoop of mint chocolate chip
ice cream and cherry
Shake with ice, strain into an Irish coffee glass, and stir.
Top with scoop of mint chocolate chip ice cream and
cherry.

LET'S MAKE IT SCHNAPPY

1 part Bombay Sapphire®
1 part peppermint schnapps
1 part soda
Splash of lemon juice
Garnish: mint spring
Muddle soda and mint sprig in a double rocks glass. Add
Bombay Sapphire®, peppermint schnapps, and lemon
juice and stir.
Garnish with mint sprig.

LIGHTS OUT

3 parts light rum
2 parts orange juice
1 part brandy
Splash of lime juice
Splash of grenadine
Shake with ice and strain into a cocktail glass.

LILACS

3 parts Lillet
1 part lime juice
Pour into a wine glass and stir.

LIMBO CALYPSO

3 parts passion fruit juice
2 parts light rum
1 part crème de banana
Splash of lime juice (freshly squeezed)
Garnish: cherry
Build on ice in a highball glass and stir.
Garnish with cherry.

LIME DAIQUIRI

2 parts sour mix
1 part light rum
Splash of lime juice
Garnish: lime wedge
Shake with ice and strain into a rocks glass. Garnish
with lime wedge.

LIMEY MARTINI

1 part gin
Splash of lime juice
Garnish: lime wedge
Build on ice in a rocks glass.
Garnish with lime wedge.

LIQUID COMA

3 parts dark rum
1 part Southern Comfort®
1 part brown crème de cacao
Shake with ice and strain into a cocktail glass.

LIQUID PANTS REMOVER

1 part tequila
Splash of triple sec
Splash of Drambuie®
Shake with ice and strain into a cocktail glass.

LITTLE BASTARD

2 parts lemonade
1 part vodka
1 part crème de cassis
Shake with ice and strain into a cocktail glass.

LITTLE, YELLOW, DIFFERENT

2 parts vodka
1 part apricot brandy
1 part triple sec
1 part crème de banana
Splash of lemon juice
Garnish: cherry
Shake with ice and strain into a cocktail glass. Garnish
with cherry.

LONG BEACH ICED TEA

2 parts sour mix

2 parts cranberry juice

1 part gin

1 part vodka

1 part rum

1 part tequila

1 part triple sec

1 part soda

Garnish: lemon wedge

Build on ice in a tall glass and stir. Garnish with lemon wedge.

LONG ISLAND ICED TEA

4 parts sour mix

1 part gin

1 part vodka

1 part rum

1 part tequila

1 part triple sec

1 part cola

Garnish: lemon wedge

Build on ice in a tall glass and stir. Garnish with lemon wedge.

LOOKING GOOD

2 parts cola

1 part Malibu Coconut Rum®

1 part sloe gin

Shake with ice and strain into a cocktail glass.

LORD BYRON

2 parts scotch

Splash of blue curaçao

Splash of sweet vermouth

Dash of bitters

Shake with ice and strain into a cocktail glass.

LORRAINE COCKTAIL

2 parts Kirschwasser

1 part Bénédictine

Splash of lime juice

Shake with ice and strain into a cocktail glass.

LOUISIANA LULLABY

2 parts dark rum

1 part Dubonnet blonde

1 part Grand Marnier®

Shake with ice and strain into a cocktail glass.

LOUISVILLE SLUGGER

1 part blackberry brandy
Splash of lemon juice
Dash of dry vermouth
Garnish: lemon twist
Shake with ice and strain into a cocktail glass. Garnish
with lemon twist.

LOVE COCKTAIL

2 parts sloe gin
1 part spiced rum
1 part raspberry liqueur
1 egg white
Shake with ice and strain into a cocktail glass.

LOVE FOR TOBY

3 parts light rum
1 part brandy
1 part cherry brandy
Splash of lime juice
Shake with ice and strain into a cocktail glass.

LOVE ITALIAN STYLE

1 part Amaretto

1 part dark rum

1 part Armagnac

Shake with ice and strain into a cocktail glass.

LOVE ME

1 part gin

1 part Dubonnet blonde

1 part Grand Marnier®

Stir with ice and strain into a cocktail glass.

LOVEABLE

3 parts peach vodka

1 part gin

1 part triple sec

Stir with ice and strain into a cocktail glass.

LOVER'S NOCTURNE

2 parts vodka

1 part Drambuie®

Dash of bitters

Shake with ice and strain into a cocktail glass.

LUCKY LADY

2 parts dark rum

2 parts cream

1 part white crème de cacao

1 part sambuca

Shake with ice and strain into a cocktail glass.

LUCKY STIFF

2 parts cranberry juice

1 part gin

1 part blue curaçao

Garnish: lime wedge

Build on ice in a highball glass and stir. Garnish with lime wedge.

LUMBERJACK

2 parts gin
1 part Southern Comfort®
1 part applejack
1 tablespoon of syrup
Stir with ice and strain into a cocktail glass.

LUXURY

2 parts gin
1 part Pimm's® No. 1
1 part crème de banana
1 part sweet vermouth
Splash of lime juice (freshly squeezed)
Dash of bitters
Stir with ice and strain into a cocktail glass.

LYNCHBURG LEMONADE

3 parts sour mix
2 parts whiskey
1 part triple sec
1 part soda
Garnish: lemon wedge

Build on ice in a tall glass and stir. Garnish with lemon wedge.

MACAROON

3 parts vodka
1 part Amaretto
1 part brown crème de cacao
Garnish: orange twist
Shake with ice and strain into a cocktail glass. Garnish
with orange twist.

MADAME BUTTERFLY

2 parts apple brandy
1 part gin
1 part Bols® Blue
Dash of dry vermouth
Garnish: lemon twist
Stir with ice and strain into a cocktail glass. Garnish
with lemon twist.

MADRAS

1 part vodka
1 part cranberry juice
1 part orange juice
Build on ice in a highball glass.

MAGNOLIA MAIDEN

2 parts bourbon
2 parts Mandarine Napoléon®
1 part club soda
1 tablespoon of syrup
Build on ice in a rocks glass and stir.

MAI TAI

4 parts sour mix
1 part light rum
1 part triple sec
1 part crème de noyaux
1 part grenadine
Garnish: orange slice and cherry
Build on ice in a tall glass and stir. Garnish with orange
slice and cherry.

MAIDEN'S BLUSH

3 parts gin
1 part triple sec
Splash of cherry brandy
Splash of lemon juice
Garnish: cherry
Stir with ice and strain into a cocktail glass. Garnish
with cherry.

MAIDEN'S DREAM

1 part gin
1 part pastis
Splash of grenadine
Stir with ice and strain into a cocktail glass.

MAJESTIC

2 parts gin
1 part crème de banana
1 part grapefruit juice
Garnish: mint sprig
Stir with ice and strain into a cocktail glass. Garnish
with mint sprig.

MAJOR TOM

1 part vodka
Splash of triple sec
Splash of Kirschwasser
Splash of grapefruit juice
Shake with ice and strain into a cocktail glass.

MAKE IT HAPPEN

1 part light rum
1 part sloe gin
1 part grenadine
1 part cream
Garnish: scoop of strawberry ice cream and
strawberry syrup
Build on ice in a highball glass. Top with scoop of
strawberry ice cream and strawberry syrup.

MALAYSIA

1 part gin
1 part cherry brandy
1 part sour mix
Garnish: lime slice
Stir with ice and strain into a cocktail glass. Garnish
with lime slice.

MALIBU BAY BREEZE

1 part Malibu Coconut Rum®
1 part cranberry juice
1 part pineapple juice
Build on ice in a highball glass.

MALIBU EXPRESS

1 part Malibu Coconut Rum®
1 part light rum
Splash of lemon-lime soda
Splash of pineapple juice
Shake with ice and strain into a cocktail glass.

MALIBU WAVE

1 part tequila
1 part blue curaçao
1 part sour mix
Garnish: lime wedge
Shake with ice and strain into a cocktail glass. Garnish
with lime wedge.

MALIBU WINNER

2 parts white wine
1 part Malibu Coconut Rum[R]
1 part sloe gin
Pour into a wine glass and stir.

MAN OF THE MOMENT

2 parts scotch
1 part Grand Marnier[R]
Splash of grenadine
Splash of lemon juice
Shake with ice and strain into a cocktail glass.

MANGO MAMA

2 parts mango juice
1 part dark rum
1 part Malibu Coconut Rum[R]
1 part peach schnapps
Shake with ice and strain into a cocktail glass.

MANHATTAN

1 part bourbon

Dash of sweet vermouth

Dash of bitters

Garnish: cherry

Muddle bitters and cherry in a rocks glass. Add ice and pour bourbon and sweet vermouth. Garnish with cherry.

MAPLE LEAF

2 parts Canadian Club® whiskey

1 part blackberry brandy

1 part grapefruit juice

Garnish: lemon twist

Shake with ice and strain into a cocktail glass. Garnish with lemon twist.

MARDI GRAS

2 parts Bacardi® light rum
1 part lime juice (freshly squeezed)
Splash of Southern Comfort®
Splash of crème de banana
Shake with ice and strain into a cocktail glass.

MARGARITA

3 parts tequila
3 parts sour mix
1 part triple sec
1 part lime juice
Garnish: salt rim and lime wedge
Rim margarita glass with lime, then dip rim in salt.
Shake tequila, triple sec, lime juice, and sour mix with
ice and strain into the salt-rimmed glass. Garnish with
lime wedge.

MARTINI

1 part gin
Dash of dry vermouth
Garnish: olive
Stir with ice and strain into a cocktail glass. Garnish
with olive.

MARTINI (VODKA)

1 part vodka
Dash of dry vermouth
Garnish: olive
Stir with ice and strain into a cocktail glass. Garnish
with olive.

MARTINI MILANO

2 parts gin
1 part Campari®
1 part white wine
Dash of dry vermouth
Garnish: lemon twist
Stir with ice and strain into a cocktail glass. Garnish
with lemon twist.

MARY PICKFORD COCKTAIL

1 part light rum
1 part pineapple juice
Splash of grenadine
Garnish: cherry
Shake with ice and strain into a cocktail glass. Garnish
with cherry.

MEDITERRANEAN DELIGHT

1 part gin
Splash of crème de banana
Splash of cranberry juice
Stir with ice and strain into a cocktail glass.

MELLOW OUT

2 parts Bailey's Irish Cream®
2 parts melon liqueur
1 part light rum
Splash of grenadine
Shake with ice and strain into a cocktail glass.

MELON BALL COCKTAIL

3 parts melon liqueur
1 part vodka
1 part orange juice
1 part pineapple juice
Build on ice in a highball glass and stir.

MELON CACAO

2 parts white crème de menthe
1 part white crème de cacao
1 part melon liqueur
Splash of lemon juice
Shake with ice and strain into a cocktail glass.

MELON CITRON

1 part Absolut® Citron
1 part grapefruit juice
Splash of melon liqueur
Splash of raspberry liqueur
Shake with ice and strain into a cocktail glass.

MELONADE

2 parts lemonade
1 part melon liqueur
Splash of lime juice (freshly squeezed)
Dash of Bacardi 151®
Shake with ice and strain into a cocktail glass.

MEMPHIS BELLE COCKTAIL

2 parts brandy
1 part Southern Comfort®
Splash of lemon juice
Dash of bitters
Shake with ice and strain into a cocktail glass.

MERRY WIDOW COCKTAIL

2 parts gin

2 parts sweet vermouth

1 part Bénédictine

1 part anisette

Dash of bitters

Garnish: lemon twist

Stir with ice and strain into a cocktail glass. Garnish with lemon twist.

MESSALINA

1 part Cognac

Splash of brown crème de cacao

Dash of bitters

Garnish: cherry

Shake with ice and strain into a cocktail glass. Garnish with cherry.

MEXICAN BESTING

1 part Jose Cuervo® tequila
Splash of pastis
Splash of white crème de menthe
Garnish: lemon twist
Shake with ice and strain into a cocktail glass. Garnish
with lemon twist.

MEXICAN CHICKEN

1 part tequila
1 egg white
Splash of hot sauce
Shake with ice and strain into a cocktail glass.

MEXICAN ICED TEA

2 parts beer
1 part tequila
Splash of lime juice
Garnish: lime wedge
Build on ice in a tall glass and stir.
Garnish with lime wedge.

MEXICAN LOVER

2 parts tequila
1 part brandy
Dash of dry vermouth
Shake with ice and strain into a cocktail glass.

MEXICAN NOG

2 parts tequila
1 part rum
1 part advocaat
Garnish: ground nutmeg
Shake with ice and strain into a cocktail glass. Garnish
with ground nutmeg.

MEXICAN ORANGE

2 parts tequila
1 part orange vodka
1 part Cointreau®
Splash of lime juice
Garnish: orange slice and cherry
Shake with ice and strain into a cocktail glass.

MIAMI COCKTAIL

3 parts rum
1 part green crème de menthe
Splash of lime juice
Shake with ice and strain into a cocktail glass.

MIAMI ICED TEA

4 parts sour mix
1 part gin
1 part vodka
1 part rum
1 part tequila
1 part blue curaçao
1 part soda
Garnish: lemon wedge
Build on ice in a tall glass and stir.
Garnish with lemon wedge.

MIDNIGHT JOY

1 part white crème de cacao
1 part black sambuca
Shake with ice and strain into a cocktail glass.

MIDNIGHT RHAPSODY

2 parts vanilla vodka
2 parts Kahlua®
1 part brown crème de cacao
1 part coffee
Garnish: whipped cream
Shake with ice and strain into a cocktail glass. Garnish
with whipped cream.

MIDNIGHT WAKEUP

3 parts hot cocoa
1 part brandy
1 part white crème de cacao
1 part white crème de menthe
1 part Bailey's Irish Cream®
Pour into an Irish coffee glass and stir.

MIDORI SOUR

2 parts sour mix
1 part Midori®
Garnish: orange slice and cherry
Shake with ice and strain into a rocks glass. Garnish
with orange slice and cherry.

MIDSUMMER NIGHT DREAM

2 parts vodka
1 part Kirschwasser
Splash of strawberry liqueur
Garnish: strawberry
Shake with ice and strain into a cocktail glass. Garnish
with strawberry.

MIKE COLLINS

3 parts sour mix

2 parts Irish whiskey

1 part soda

Garnish: orange slice and cherry

Build on ice in a tall glass and stir. Garnish with orange slice and cherry.

MILK AND HONEY

3 parts Irish Mist®

1 part Bailey's Irish Cream®

Build on ice in a rocks glass.

MILKY WAY MARTINI

2 parts vanilla vodka

2 parts chocolate liqueur

1 part Bailey's Irish Cream®

Shake with ice and strain into a cocktail glass.

MILLION DOLLAR COCKTAIL

2 parts gin
1 part sweet vermouth
1 part grenadine
1 part pineapple juice
1 egg white
Stir with ice and strain into a cocktail glass.

MIMOSA

1 part champagne
1 part orange juice
Pour into a champagne flute.

MIND BENDER

2 parts gin
1 part plum brandy
Splash of orange juice
Stir with ice and strain into a cocktail glass.

MINT COFFEE

1 part peppermint schnapps
1 part Tia Maria®
Shake with ice and strain into a cocktail glass.

MINT CREAM PIE

1 part Bailey's Irish Cream®
1 part sambuca
1 part green crème de menthe
1 part cream
Shake with ice and strain into a cocktail glass.

MINT GIN MARTINI

1 part gin
1 part white wine
Splash of peppermint schnapps
Dash of dry vermouth
Stir with ice and strain into a cocktail glass.

MINT GLACIER

3 parts vodka
1 part Absolut® Citron
1 part green crème de menthe
Shake with ice and strain into a cocktail glass.

MINT JULEP

3 parts bourbon
1 part green crème de menthe
1 tablespoon of sugar
Garnish: mint sprig
Muddle green crème de menthe, sugar,
and mint sprig in a highball glass.
Add bourbon and ice and stir.

MINT LEMONADE

2 parts sparkling wine
1 part white crème de menthe
1 part lemonade
Garnish: mint sprig
Pour into a wine glass and stir. Garnish with mint sprig.

MINT MAYFAIR

1 part gin
Splash of lime juice (freshly squeezed)
Tablespoon of syrup
Garnish: cucumber slices and mint sprig
Muddle cucumber, mint sprig, and lime juice in a mixing glass. Add gin and ice, shake, and strain into a cocktail glass.

MINT MONKEY

1 part brandy
1 part crème de banana
1 part Bols® Chocolate Mint
Shake with ice and strain into a cocktail glass.

MINT PUNCH

2 parts Bacardi® dark rum

1 part crème de banana

1 part sweet vermouth

1 part peppermint schnapps

Splash of pineapple juice

Garnish: mint sprig

Shake with ice and strain into a double rocks glass.

Garnish with mint sprig.

MINT ROYALE

1 part brandy

1 part Bols® Chocolate Mint

1 egg white

Shake with ice and strain into a cocktail glass.

MINT SUNRISE

3 parts scotch

1 part brandy

1 part blue curaçao

Garnish: mint sprig

Muddle scotch and mint sprig in a rocks glass. Add
brandy and blue curaçao and stir.

MINTY FIZZ

2 parts lemon–lime soda

1 part dark rum

1 part peppermint schnapps

Splash of lime juice (freshly squeezed)

Shake with ice and strain into a double rocks glass.

MIRAGE

3 parts cola

1 part vodka

1 part Jack Daniel's®

Build on ice in a highball glass and stir.

MISCHIEF NIGHT

2 parts vodka

1 part apple juice

1 part grapefruit juice

Garnish: lemon wedge

Build on ice in a highball glass and stir. Garnish with lemon wedge.

MISS BELLE

3 parts dark rum

1 part Grand Marnier®

1 part brown crème de cacao

Shake with ice and strain into a cocktail glass.

MISS MARTINI

2 parts vodka
1 part crème de cerise
1 part raspberry liqueur
1 part cream
Pinch of sugar
Dash of bitters
Shake with ice and strain into a cocktail glass.

MISSISSIPPI MULE

1 part gin
Splash of crème de cassis
Splash of lemon juice
Stir with ice and strain into a cocktail glass.

MISSOURI MULE

3 parts bourbon
1 part crème de cassis
Splash of cola
Garnish: cherry
Shake with ice and strain into a cocktail glass. Garnish
with cherry.

MISTAKE

1 part peppermint schnapps
1 part soda
Garnish: lemon slice
Shake with ice and strain into a cocktail glass. Garnish
with lemon slice.

MISTLETOE

1 part gin
1 part grenadine
Splash of lemon juice
Splash of cranberry juice
Stir with ice and strain into a cocktail glass.

MISTY SUNSET

1 part peach schnapps

1 part triple sec

1 part grenadine

1 part cranberry juice

Shake with ice and strain into a cocktail glass.

MOAT FLOAT

3 parts cola

1 part vodka

1 part Amaretto

Garnish: cherry

Build on ice in a highball glass and stir.

Garnish with cherry.

MOCHA ALEXANDER

1 part brandy
1 part coffee liqueur
1 part cream
Garnish: ground nutmeg
Shake with ice and strain into a cocktail glass. Garnish
with ground nutmeg.

MOCHA MARTINI

3 parts vodka
1 part Kahlua®
1 part white crème de cacao
Garnish: chocolate syrup rim
Shake with ice and strain into a chocolate-rimmed
cocktail glass.

MOCHA MINT

1 part coffee brandy
1 part white crème de menthe
1 part white crème de cacao
Shake with ice and strain into a cocktail glass.

MODERN SHERRY

1 part gin
1 part cream sherry
Stir with ice and strain into a cocktail glass.

MODUS OPERANDI

2 parts vodka
2 parts light rum
1 part triple sec
1 part melon liqueur
1 part pineapple juice
Garnish: lemon twist
Shake with ice and strain into a cocktail glass. Garnish
with lemon twist.

MOGAMBO

2 parts vodka

1 part cream

1 tablespoon of chocolate syrup

Splash of cherry brandy

Garnish: cinnamon stick

Shake with ice and strain into a cocktail glass. Garnish with cinnamon stick.

MOJITO

3 parts light rum

2 parts soda

1 tablespoon of sugar

Garnish: 3 mint sprigs, 3 lime wedges

Muddle sugar, mint sprigs, and lime wedges in a tall glass. Add ice, rum, and soda and stir.

MOLL MARTINI

2 parts sloe gin
1 part gin
Dash of dry vermouth
Stir with ice and strain into a cocktail glass.

MOMBASA

2 parts grapefruit juice
2 parts pineapple juice
1 part light rum
1 part crème de cassis
Splash of sweet vermouth
Shake with ice and strain into a cocktail glass.

MON AMI

1 part Armagnac
Splash of peppermint schnapps
Splash of pastis
Garnish: cherry
Shake with ice and strain into a cocktail glass. Garnish
with cherry.

MON AMOUR

2 parts Bols® Genever
1 part sake
Splash of crème de violette
Splash of orange juice
Shake with ice and strain into a cocktail glass.

MONDO

2 parts grapefruit juice
1 part vodka
1 part crème de cassis
Build on ice in a highball glass and stir.

MONK'S MARTINI

1 part vodka
1 part Bailey's Irish Cream®
1 part white crème de menthe
1 part crème de banana
Shake with ice and strain into a cocktail glass.

MONKEY GLAND COCKTAIL

2 parts gin

1 part orange juice

Splash of Bénédictine

Splash of crème de banana

Stir with ice and strain into a cocktail glass.

MONKEY MIX

2 parts cranberry juice

1 part crème de banana

1 part raspberry liqueur

Splash of grenadine

Build on ice in a highball glass and stir.

MONKEY SEE MONKEY DO

1 part crème de banana

1 part rum

1 part orange Juice

Shake with ice and strain into a cocktail glass.

MONTEGO BAY

2 parts Kahlua®
1 part Bacardi® dark rum
1 part crème de banana
2 scoops of vanilla ice cream
Garnish: whipped cream

Mix in a blender and pour into a highball glass. Garnish with whipped cream.

MONTMARTRE

1 part brandy
Splash of blue curaçao
Splash of sweet vermouth
Garnish: cherry

Shake with ice and strain into a cocktail glass. Garnish with cherry.

MONTREAL AFTER DARK

1 part whiskey
1 part white crème de cacao

Shake with ice and strain into a cocktail glass.

MOO MOO LAND

2 parts cream
1 part dark rum
1 part crème de banana
Splash of grenadine
Garnish: ground nutmeg
Shake with ice and strain into a cocktail glass. Garnish with ground nutmeg.

MOON QUAKE SHAKE

2 parts dark rum
1 part apricot brandy
1 part plum brandy
Splash of lemon juice
Shake with ice and strain into a cocktail glass.

MOON ROCK

2 parts Parfait Amour
1 part vodka
Dash of dry vermouth
Shake with ice and strain into a cocktail glass.

MOONBEAM

1 part blue curaçao
1 part white crème de cacao
Splash of orange juice
Shake with ice and strain into a cocktail glass.

MOON GLOW

1 part brandy
1 part peppermint schnapps
Shake with ice and strain into a cocktail glass.

MOONLIGHT COCKTAIL

1 part gin
1 part white wine
1 part Kirschwasser
Splash of grapefruit juice
Stir with ice and strain into a wine glass.

MOONLIGHT DRIVE

2 parts orange juice
2 parts pineapple juice
1 part Malibu Coconut Rum®
1 part rum
1 part vodka
1 part sloe gin
1 part Amaretto
Build on ice in a highball glass and stir.

MOONSHINE BELLS

1 part triple sec
1 part crème de cassis
Splash of lime juice (freshly squeezed)
Garnish: orange slice
Shake with ice and strain into a cocktail glass. Garnish
with orange slice.

MOONSHINE COCKTAIL

1 part brandy
1 part Dubonnet blonde
1 part peach schnapps
Dash of pastis
Shake with ice and strain into a cocktail glass.

MOOSE RIVER HUMMER

1 part Galliano®
1 part light rum
1 part whiskey
1 part Rumple Minze®
Shake with ice and strain into a cocktail glass.

MORE FUN THAN A BARREL OF MONKEYS

1 part brown crème de cacao
1 part crème de cassis
1 part Bailey's Irish Cream®
Shake with ice and strain into a cocktail glass.

MORGAN'S MOUNTAIN

1 part light rum
1 part white crème de cacao
1 part coffee liqueur
1 part vanilla milk
Shake with ice and strain into a cocktail glass.

MORNING COCKTAIL

1 part brandy
1 part triple sec
1 part anisette
Dash of dry vermouth
Dash of bitters
Garnish: cherry
Shake with ice and strain into a cocktail glass. Garnish
with cherry.

MORNING JOY

2 parts gin

1 part peach schnapps

1 part orange juice

Garnish: orange slice

Stir with ice and strain into a cocktail glass. Garnish with orange slice.

MORNING ROSE

1 part Bacardi® light rum

1 part blue curaçao

1 part orange juice

Splash of grenadine

Shake with ice and strain into a cocktail glass.

MOSCOW DAWN

2 parts vodka
1 part peppermint schnapps
1 part triple sec
Garnish: mint sprig
Pour into a wine glass and stir. Garnish with mint sprig.

MOSCOW SNOW

1 part vodka
1 part white crème de cacao
Garnish: ground nutmeg
Shake with ice and strain into a cocktail glass. Garnish
with ground nutmeg.

MOTHER OF PEARL

1 part gin
1 part anisette
Stir with ice and strain into a cocktail glass.

MOTHER TONGUE

1 part crème de banana
1 part Bols® Red Orange
1 part Bacardi® light rum
Pinch of sugar
Shake with ice and strain into a cocktail glass.

MOULIN ROUGE

2 parts sloe gin
1 part sweet vermouth
1 part ginger ale
Dash of bitters
Shake with ice and strain into a cocktail glass.

MOUNDS

1 part chocolate vodka
1 part Malibu Coconut Rum®
Garnish: chocolate syrup rim
Shake with ice and strain into a chocolate-rimmed
cocktail glass.

MOUNTAIN COCKTAIL

1 part whiskey

1 egg white

Splash of lemon juice

Dash of dry vermouth

Dash of sweet vermouth

Shake with ice and strain into a cocktail glass.

MOUSSE CHERRY

1 part vodka

1 part cherry brandy

1 part grapefruit juice

Shake with ice and strain into a cocktail glass.

MOZART

1 part añejo rum
Splash of sweet vermouth
Splash of triple sec
Dash of bitters
Garnish: lemon twist
Shake with ice and strain into a cocktail glass. Garnish
with lemon twist.

MR. DRY

1 part apricot brandy
1 part Aperol
1 part peach juice
Dash of dry vermouth
Shake with ice and strain into a cocktail glass.

MR. MANHATTAN

2 parts gin
1 part orange juice
1 part soda
Pinch of sugar
Garnish: mint sprig
Muddle mint sprig with the club soda and sugar in a
wine glass. Shake gin and orange juice with ice and
strain into the wine glass.

MR. NEW YORK

1 part gin
1 part sherry
Splash of sweet vermouth
Splash of triple sec
Stir with ice and strain into a cocktail glass.

MUDDY WATERS

2 parts cherry cola
1 part vodka
1 part Bailey's Irish Cream®
1 part chocolate liqueur
Build on ice in a highball glass and stir.

MUDSLIDE

2 parts cream
1 part vodka
1 part Bailey's Irish Cream®
1 part Kahlua®
Shake with ice and strain into a cocktail glass.

MULCH MUNCHER

2 parts vodka
1 part Strega®
Splash of crème de banana
Splash of orange juice
Shake with ice and strain into a cocktail glass.

MULE'S HIND LEG

1 part brandy
1 part Bénédictine
1 part gin
1 tablespoon of syrup
Stir with ice and strain into a cocktail glass.

MUMSICLE

1 part dark rum
Dash of bitters
Garnish: cherry
Shake with ice and strain into a cocktail glass. Garnish with cherry.

MUTINY

3 parts dark rum
1 part Dubonnet rouge
Dash of bitters
Garnish: cherry
Shake with ice and strain into a cocktail glass. Garnish with cherry.

MUTZIPUTZI

2 parts peach juice
1 part Bacardi® Limon
1 part Campari®
1 part Aperol
1 part orange juice
1 part pineapple juice
Garnish: peach slice

Build on ice in a tall glass and stir. Garnish with peach slice.

MUY MAL

1 part añejo rum
Dash of dry vermouth
Dash of grenadine
Garnish: cherry

Shake with ice and strain into a cocktail glass. Garnish with cherry.

MVP

2 parts vodka

2 parts pineapple juice

1 part Midori®

1 part Malibu Coconut Rum®

Build on ice in a tall glass and stir.

MY VALENTINE

2 parts cranberry juice

1 part pineapple juice

1 part Malibu Coconut Rum®

1 part Midori®

Shake with ice and strain into a cocktail glass.

NAIL BITER

2 parts pineapple juice
1 part vodka
1 part root beer schnapps
Shake with ice and strain into a cocktail glass.

NAKED TWISTER

3 parts pineapple juice
2 parts Midori®
1 part vodka
1 part Tuaca®
Garnish: cherry
Build on ice in a tall glass and stir.
Garnish with cherry.

NAKED WAITER

3 parts lemonade
1 part Mandarine Napoléon®
1 part pastis
1 part pineapple Juice
Garnish: lemon slice
Build on ice in a tall glass and stir. Garnish with lemon slice.

NAPOLEON

2 parts gin
1 part blue curaçao
1 part Dubonnet blonde
Stir with ice and strain into a cocktail glass.

NATURE

1 part tequila
1 part peach schnapps
1 part peppermint schnapps
Shake with ice and strain into a cocktail glass.

NAVEL RAZZ

1 part vodka

1 part raspberry liqueur

1 part orange juice

Shake with ice and strain into a cocktail glass.

NEGRONI

1 part gin

1 part Campari®

1 part sweet vermouth

Garnish: orange slice

Stir with ice and strain into a cocktail glass. Garnish with orange slice.

NEON GREEN

2 parts lemon–lime soda

1 part Malibu Coconut Rum®

1 part melon liqueur

1 part peppermint schnapps

Build on ice in a tall glass and stir.

NEON IGUANA

2 parts spiced rum
2 parts orange juice
1 part Malibu Coconut Rum®
1 part blue curaçao
Splash of lime juice
Build on ice in a tall glass and stir.

NEAPOLITAN

2 parts vodka
1 part Cointreau®
1 part Chambord®
1 part cranberry juice
Garnish: lemon twist
Shake with ice and strain into a cocktail glass. Garnish
with lemon twist.

NET SURFER

1 part Cognac
1 part vodka
1 part peach schnapps
1 part orange juice
Splash of lemon juice
Garnish: strawberry syrup rim
Shake with ice and strain into a strawberry syrup-
rimmed cocktail glass.

NETWORK SPECIAL

2 parts light rum
1 part coffee liqueur
1 part cream
Dash of Bacardi® 151
Shake with ice and strain into a cocktail glass.

NEVER AGAIN

2 parts bourbon

Splash of sweet vermouth

Splash of pastis

Garnish: lemon twist

Shake with ice and strain into a cocktail glass. Garnish
with lemon twist.

NEVER LET ME DOWN

2 parts triple sec

1 part lemonade

1 part lemon-lime soda

Splash of grenadine

Shake with ice and strain into a cocktail glass.

NEW ORLEANS COCKTAIL

3 parts bourbon
1 part pastis
1 tablespoon of syrup
Splash of anisette
Dash of bitters
Garnish: Lemon twist

Shake with ice and strain into a cocktail glass. Garnish with lemon twist.

NEW ORLEANS MARTINI

1 part vanilla vodka
Splash of dry vermouth
Splash of pastis
Garnish: mint sprig

Shake with ice and strain into a cocktail glass. Garnish with mint sprig.

NEW YORK LEMONADE

2 parts Absolut® Citron
2 parts lemon juice
1 part Grand Marnier®
1 part soda
Garnish: sugar rim

Shake with ice and strain into a sugar-rimmed cocktail glass.

NEW YORK SLAPPER

2 parts vodka
2 parts Tia Maria®
2 parts cream
1 part Amaretto

Shake with ice and strain into a cocktail glass.

NEW YORK, NEW YORK

1 part whiskey
1 tablespoon of syrup
Splash of grenadine
Garnish: orange twist
Shake with ice and strain into a cocktail glass. Garnish
with orange twist.

NIAGARA FALLS

2 parts champagne
1 part Mandarine Napoléon®
Pinch of sugar
Pour into a champagne flute and stir.

NIGHT CAP COCKTAIL

1 part brandy
1 part blue curaçao
1 egg white
Dash of Amer Picon®
Shake with ice and strain into a cocktail glass.

NIGHT NIGHT

1 part brandy

1 part brown crème de cacao

Splash of triple sec

Splash of coffee liqueur

Shake with ice and strain into a cocktail glass.

NIGHT STARS

1 part brandy

1 part crème de banana

Splash of whiskey

Splash of blue curaçao

Splash of apple juice

Garnish: Cherry

Shake with ice and strain into a cocktail glass. Garnish
with cherry.

NIGHT TRAIN

3 parts coffee
1 part vodka
1 part Frangelico®
1 tablespoon of syrup
Garnish: coffee beans
Pour into an Irish coffee glass and stir. Garnish with
coffee beans.

NIGHTMARE

3 parts gin
1 part Madeira
1 part cherry brandy
Splash of orange juice
Stir with ice and strain into a cocktail glass.

NINETEEN

1 part gin

Splash of Kirschwasser

Dash of pastis

Dash of dry vermouth

Pinch of sugar

Stir with ice and strain into a cocktail glass.

NINETEEN TWENTY

1 part gin

1 part Kirschwasser

Splash of pastis

Dash of dry vermouth

Stir with ice and strain into a cocktail glass.

NINOTCHKA

1 part vodka

1 part butterscotch schnapps

1 part ginger liqueur

Shake with ice and strain into a cocktail glass.

NITRO COCKTAIL

2 parts vodka
2 parts scotch whiskey
1 part cranberry juice
1 part orange juice
Splash of grenadine
Build on ice in a double rocks glass and stir.

NITWIT

1 part mezcal
1 part vodka
1 part Southern Comfort®
1 part orange juice
Shake with ice and strain into a cocktail glass.

NO SAINT

1 part vodka
1 part orange juice
Dash of dry vermouth
Dash of bitters
Shake with ice and strain into a cocktail glass.

NOCHE

2 parts pineapple juice
2 parts cranberry juice
1 part vodka
1 part light rum
1 part bourbon
Splash of melon liqueur
Garnish: cherry
Build on ice in a tall glass and stir.
Garnish with cherry.

NOIR GRAND

2 parts red wine
1 part Grand Marnier®
Garnish: orange slices
Pour into a wine glass and stir.
Garnish with orange slices.

NOMAD

1 part Cointreau®
1 part Midori®
1 part sour mix
Shake with ice and strain into a cocktail glass.

NORDIC SEA

2 parts gin
2 parts pineapple juice
1 part Bols® Kiwi
Splash of Bols® Blue
Garnish: cherry
Build on ice in a highball glass and stir.
Garnish with cherry.

NORMANDY GOLDEN DAWN

1 part gin
1 part apricot brandy
1 part iced tea
Splash of grenadine
Stir with ice and strain into a cocktail glass.

NORTH POLE COCKTAIL

1 part gin

1 part lemon juice

1 egg white

Garnish: whipped cream and cherry

Stir with ice and strain into a cocktail glass. Garnish
with whipped cream and cherry.

NORTHERN EXPOSURE

1 part gin

1 part peach schnapps

1 part triple sec

Splash of lemon juice

Stir with ice and strain into a cocktail glass.

NORTHERN SKY

1 part gin

1 part Cointreau®

1 part Campari®

Stir with ice and strain into a cocktail glass.

NORWEGIAN SUMMER

1 part dark rum
1 part apricot brandy
1 part peppermint schnapps
Splash of sweet vermouth
Splash of lime juice (freshly squeezed)
Shake with ice and strain into a cocktail glass.

NOTHING LIKE IT

1 part sweet vermouth
1 part Kirschwasser
Splash of grenadine
Splash of orange juice
Shake with ice and strain into a cocktail glass.

NOUGAT ICE CREAM

1 part vanilla vodka
1 part hazelnut liqueur
1 part cream
Shake with ice and strain into a cocktail glass.

NOW THIS IS FUN

1 part gin
1 part raspberry liqueur
Dash of dry vermouth
Dash of bitters
Stir with ice and strain into a cocktail glass.

NSFW

2 parts Licor 43®
1 part light rum
1 egg white
Shake with ice and strain into a cocktail glass.

NUCLEAR ICED TEA

2 parts melon liqueur
2 parts cranberry juice
1 part vodka
1 part gin
1 part rum
1 part triple sec
Build on ice in a tall glass and stir.

NUDIST COLONY

1 part gin
1 part Cognac
1 part Dubonnet blonde
1 part Chartreuse
Shake with ice and strain into a cocktail glass.

NUTS AND BERRIES

2 parts cream
1 part Frangelico®
1 part raspberry schnapps
Shake with ice and strain into a cocktail glass.

NUTTY COMBO

2 parts beer
1 part Amaretto
Build on ice in a tall glass and stir.

NUTTY IRISHMAN

3 parts Bailey's Irish Cream®
1 part Frangelico®
Build on ice in a rocks glass.

NUTTY MARTINI

1 part vodka
Splash of Frangelico®
Shake with ice and strain into a cocktail glass.

NUTTY STINGER

2 parts Amaretto
1 part white crème de menthe
Shake with ice and strain into a cocktail glass.

NUTTY WAKEUP CALL

1 part whiskey
1 part coffee brandy
Splash of Amaretto
Splash of hazelnut liqueur
Shake with ice and strain into a cocktail glass.

OAK TREE

2 parts chocolate milk
1 part brandy
1 part Amaretto
1 part Tia Maria®
Build on ice in a tall glass and stir.

OASIS OF PEACE

2 parts white crème de cacao
2 parts crème de banana
1 part cream
1 part vanilla milk
Shake with ice and strain into a cocktail glass.

OATMEAL COOKIE

3 parts butterscotch schnapps
3 parts Bailey's Irish Cream®
Splash of Jägermeister®
Splash of cinnamon schnapps
Shake with ice and strain into a rocks glass.

OCEAN DRIVE

2 parts Malibu Coconut Rum®
1 part blue curaçao
Splash of orange juice
Splash of pineapple juice
Splash of cranberry juice
Shake with ice and strain into a cocktail glass.

ODESSA PEACH

2 parts peach brandy
1 part vodka
Splash of triple sec
Splash of Chartreuse
Shake with ice and strain into a cocktail glass.

OFF THE BOAT

2 parts tequila

2 parts coconut brandy

1 part cream

Shake with ice and strain into a cocktail glass.

OFF-WHITE

1 part Malibu Coconut Rum®

1 part vanilla vodka

1 part Amaretto

Shake with ice and strain into a cocktail glass.

OLD CAR

1 part vodka

1 part apple brandy

1 part grapefruit juice

Splash of blue curaçao

Shake with ice and strain into a cocktail glass.

OLD COUNTRY MARTINI

2 parts vodka

1 part Kirschwasser

1 part Madeira

Shake with ice and strain into a cocktail glass.

OLD FASHIONED

1 part whiskey

1 tablespoon of sugar

Splash of soda

Dash of bitters

Garnish: orange slice and cherry

Muddle bitters and sugar in a rocks glass.

Add ice and pour whiskey and soda.

Garnish with orange slice and cherry.

OLD PAL

1 part whiskey

1 part Campari®

Dash of dry vermouth

Shake with ice and strain into a cocktail glass.

OLD SCHOOL FLAVOR

2 parts gin
2 parts crème de banana
Splash of sweet vermouth
Splash of Campari®
Shake with ice and strain into a cocktail glass.

OLÉ

2 parts tequila
1 part coffee liqueur
1 part cream
1 tablespoon of syrup
Shake with ice and strain into a cocktail glass.

OLYMPIC GOLD

1 part apple schnapps
1 part cinnamon schnapps
1 part pineapple juice
1 part apple juice
Garnish: pineapple slice
Shake with ice and strain into a cocktail glass. Garnish
with pineapple slice.

ON SAFARI

2 parts cranberry juice
1 part whiskey
1 part cherry brandy
1 part Safari®
1 part orange juice
Build on ice in a tall glass and stir.

ON THE BEACH

2 parts cranberry juice
1 part vodka
1 part Chambord®
1 part orange juice
Build on ice in a highball glass and stir.

ON THE DECK

3 parts spiced rum
1 part cranberry juice
Splash of Cointreau®
Shake with ice and strain into a cocktail glass.

ON THE EDGE

1 part vodka
1 part white crème de cacao
1 part black sambuca
1 part cream
Shake with ice and strain into a cocktail glass.

ON THE LOOSE

2 parts light rum

1 part triple sec

1 part cherry brandy

1 part pineapple juice

Shake with ice and strain into a cocktail glass.

ON THE SLY

2 parts Campari®

1 part Strega®

1 part tonic water

Shake with ice and strain into a cocktail glass.

ONCE UPON A TIME

2 parts vodka

1 part crème de cassis

1 part apricot brandy

Splash of lime juice

Shake with ice and strain into a cocktail glass.

ONE MORE PLEASE

2 parts pineapple juice

1 part scotch

1 part pastis

Garnish: sugar rim

Shake with ice and strain into a sugar-rimmed
cocktail glass.

ONLY IN A DREAM

1 part orange juice

1 part pineapple juice

1 part peach schnapps

1 part Southern Comfort®

Build on ice in a tall glass and stir.

OPERA

2 parts Dubonnet blonde

1 part gin

1 part sloe gin

Stir with ice and strain into a cocktail glass.

ORANGE CLIMAX

2 parts whiskey
1 part peach schnapps
1 part pineapple juice
1 part orange juice
Shake with ice and strain into a cocktail glass.

ORANGE CLOCKWORK

2 parts Absolut® Mandarin
1 part triple sec
1 part orange juice
Splash of lime juice (freshly squeezed)
Shake with ice and strain into a cocktail glass.

ORANGE COMFORT

2 parts Southern Comfort®
1 part lemon juice
1 part orange juice
Splash of sambuca
Shake with ice and strain into a cocktail glass.

ORANGE HURRICANE

1 part apricot brandy

1 part blue curaçao

1 part orange juice

Dash of bitters

Shake with ice and strain into a cocktail glass.

ORANGE TRUFFLE

2 parts orange vodka

1 part chocolate liqueur

1 part cream

Garnish: chocolate syrup rim

Shake with ice and strain into a chocolate-rimmed
cocktail glass.

ORCHIDS

1 part Cognac

1 part whiskey

1 part coffee liqueur

Shake with ice and strain into a cocktail glass.

ORGASMATRON

2 parts chocolate milk
1 part sloe gin
1 part white crème de cacao
1 part advocaat
Shake with ice and strain into a cocktail glass.

ORIENTAL

1 part whiskey
Splash of triple sec
Splash of lime juice
Dash of sweet vermouth
Shake with ice and strain into a cocktail glass.

ORIGINAL SIN

2 parts champagne
1 part brandy
Splash of triple sec
Splash of grenadine
Pour into a brandy snifter and stir.

ORO

2 parts spiced rum

1 part advocaat

1 part brown crème de cacao

Shake with ice and strain into a cocktail glass.

OSAKA DRY

3 parts vodka

1 part sake

Shake with ice and strain into a cocktail glass.

OYSTER BAY

2 parts pineapple juice

1 part dark rum

1 part anisette

1 tablespoon of syrup

Splash of lime juice (freshly squeezed)

Shake with ice and strain into a cocktail glass.

PACE FEELER

2 parts vodka

1 part triple sec

1 part crème de cassis

Shake with ice and strain into a cocktail glass.

PACIFIST

1 part light rum

1 part brandy

1 part raspberry liqueur

Splash of lemon juice

Shake with ice and strain into a cocktail glass.

PAGO PAGO

1 part light rum
1 part white crème de cacao
1 part Chartreuse
Splash of lime juice
Splash of pineapple juice
Shake with ice and strain into a cocktail glass.

PAGODA

2 parts tomato juice
1 part gin
1 part sake
Splash of soy sauce
Pinch of salt
Build on ice in a tall glass and stir.

PALE MARTINI

2 parts vodka

1 part peppermint schnapps

Dash of dry vermouth

Dash of sweet vermouth

Shake with ice and strain into a cocktail glass.

PALM BEACH

2 parts gin

1 part cherry schnapps

1 part grapefruit juice

Stir with ice and strain into a cocktail glass.

PALM TREE STRUCK BY LIGHTENING

2 parts sparkling wine

1 part coconut rum

1 part pineapple juice

Pour into a wine glass and stir.

PALOMA

2 parts tequila

1 part tonic water

1 part grapefruit juice

Splash of lime juice

Shake with ice and strain into a cocktail glass.

PAMAWINE

2 parts white wine

1 part Pama®

Splash of grenadine

Pour into a wine glass and stir.

PANAMA COCKTAIL

1 part plum brandy

1 part white crème de cacao

1 part cream

Shake with ice and strain into a cocktail glass.

PANAMA LADY

2 parts cream
1 part vanilla vodka
1 part Kahlua®
1 part green crème de menthe
Shake with ice and strain into a cocktail glass.

PANCHO VILLA

1 part apricot brandy
1 part cherry schnapps
Splash of gin
Splash of light rum
Splash of pineapple juice
Stir with ice and strain into a cocktail glass.

PANDA

1 part gin
1 part plum brandy
1 part orange juice
1 tablespoon of syrup
Stir with ice and strain into a cocktail glass.

PANDORA'S BOX

2 parts gin
1 part white wine
1 part Frangelico®
Garnish: lemon twist

Stir with ice and strain into a cocktail glass. Garnish with lemon twist.

PANSY BLOSSOM COCKTAIL

1 part anisette
1 part grenadine

Shake with ice and strain into a cocktail glass.

PANTY DROPPER

1 part Bailey's Irish Cream®
1 part Pisang Ambon®
1 part cream

Shake with ice and strain into a cocktail glass.

PARADISE BAY

2 parts pineapple juice
1 part apple brandy
1 part crème de banana
Shake with ice and strain into a cocktail glass.

PARADISE ISLAND

2 parts pineapple juice
1 part gin
1 part triple sec
1 part peach schnapps
Splash of lime juice (freshly squeezed)
Shake with ice and strain into a cocktail glass.

PARALYZER

3 parts cola
1 part tequila
1 part vodka
1 part coffee liqueur
1 part cream
Build on ice in a tall glass and stir.

PARIS LOVE

1 part Armagnac
1 part cherry schnapps
1 part pineapple juice
Shake with ice and strain into a cocktail glass.

PARISIAN

1 part gin
Splash of crème de noyaux
Dash of dry vermouth
Stir with ice and strain into a cocktail glass.

PARISIAN BLONDE

1 part dark rum
1 part triple sec
1 part cream
Shake with ice and strain into a cocktail glass.

PARTY FAVOR

2 parts chocolate vodka
1 part crème de banana
1 part orange juice
Shake with ice and strain into a cocktail glass.

PARTY GIRL

2 parts cranberry juice
1 part Absolut® Kurant
1 part Chambord®
Garnish: cranberries
Build on ice in a highball glass and stir. Garnish with
cranberries.

PASSIONATE GIRL

1 part bourbon
1 part Amaretto
1 part cranberry juice
Shake with ice and strain into a cocktail glass.

PASSIONATE KISS

1 part gin
1 part Passoã®
Splash of grenadine
Stir with ice and strain into a cocktail glass.

PASSPORT TO JOY

1 part Frangelico®
1 part sloe gin
1 part cream
Shake with ice and strain into a cocktail glass.

PASTIS FRAPPE

1 part pastis
1 part sambuca
Dash of bitters
Shake with ice and strain into a cocktail glass.

PEACEFUL SEAS

1 part whiskey
1 part brown crème de cacao
1 part vanilla liqueur
Shake with ice and strain into a cocktail glass.

PEACH ALEXANDER

2 parts brandy
1 part white crème de cacao
1 part peach juice
Shake with ice and strain into a cocktail glass.

PEACH BOMBER

1 part vodka
1 part peach schnapps
1 part pineapple juice
1 part orange juice
Shake with ice and strain into a cocktail glass.

PEACH BUNNY

1 part peach schnapps

1 part white crème de cacao

1 part cream

Shake with ice and strain into a cocktail glass.

PEACH CHANDY

2 parts sparkling wine

1 part peach vodka

1 part lime juice

Pour into a wine glass and stir.

PEACH MARGARITA

2 parts sour mix

1 part tequila

1 part peach schnapps

Splash of grenadine

Shake with ice and strain into a cocktail glass.

PEACH PARTY

1 part Absolut® Kurant
1 part peach schnapps
Splash of cranberry juice
Shake with ice and strain into a cocktail glass.

PEACH SODA

2 parts lemon-lime soda
1 part peach vodka
Splash of triple sec
Build on ice in a highball glass and stir.

PEACH SPARKLER

2 parts sparkling wine
1 part peach schnapps
Splash of grenadine
Garnish: sugar rim
Pour into a sugar-rimmed wine glass and stir.

PEACHY CREAM

2 parts Bailey's Irish Cream®
1 part peach schnapps
1 part cream
Garnish: scoop of vanilla ice cream
Shake with ice and strain into a cocktail glass.
Top with vanilla ice cream

PEACHY KEEN

3 parts vodka
1 part peach schnapps
1 part lemon–lime soda
Splash of Amaretto
Shake with ice and strain into a cocktail glass.

PEACOCK

1 part white crème de cacao
1 part Parfait Amour
1 part blue curaçao
Splash of cream
Shake with ice and strain into a cocktail glass.

PEANUT BUTTER CUP

1 part chocolate vodka
1 part peanut liqueur
1 part white crème de cacao
1 part cream
Shake with ice and strain into a cocktail glass.

PECKERHEAD

2 parts orange juice
1 part Southern Comfort®
1 part vodka
1 part sloe gin
Splash of lime juice
Shake with ice and strain into a cocktail glass.

PEDRO COLLINS

3 parts sour mix
2 parts rum
1 part soda
Garnish: orange slice and cherry
Build on ice in a tall glass and stir. Garnish with orange
slice and cherry.

PEEK IN PANDORA'S BOX

2 parts ginger ale
1 part scotch
Splash of Campari®
Splash of Strega®
Shake with ice and strain into a cocktail glass.

PEKING EXPRESS

1 part gin
1 part peppermint schnapps
1 part triple sec
1 egg white
Stir with ice and strain into a cocktail glass.

PENGUIN

1 part gin
1 part Bénédictine
1 part crème de cassis
Stir with ice and strain into a cocktail glass.

PEPPERMINT COCKTAIL

1 part peppermint schnapps
1 part Cognac
Dash of dry vermouth
Shake with ice and strain into a cocktail glass.

PEPPERMINT TWIST

1 part Kahlua®
1 part brown crème de cacao
1 part peppermint schnapps
1 part strawberry milk
Shake with ice and strain into a cocktail glass.

PERFECT KILT

3 parts scotch
1 part sweet vermouth
1 part dry vermouth
Dash of bitters
Shake with ice and strain into a cocktail glass.

PERFECT MANHATTAN

1 part bourbon
Dash of dry vermouth
Dash of sweet vermouth
Garnish: cherry
Shake with ice and strain into a cocktail glass. Garnish
with cherry.

PERFECT POISON

2 parts cranberry juice

1 part Absolut® Citron

1 part Midori®

1 part triple sec

Shake with ice and strain into a cocktail glass. Garnish
with cherry.

PERFECT ROB ROY

1 part scotch

Dash of dry vermouth

Dash of sweet vermouth

Garnish: lemon twist

Stir with ice and strain into a cocktail glass. Garnish
with lemon twist.

PERFECT STORM

2 parts pineapple juice
1 part Kahlua®
1 part strawberry liqueur
Splash of cream
Garnish: scoop of strawberry ice cream
Build on ice in a highball glass and stir.
Top with scoop of strawberry ice cream.

PERFECT STRANGER

1 part dark rum
1 part crème de cassis
Splash of cola
Shake with ice and strain into a cocktail glass.

PERSIAN DELIGHT

2 parts vodka
1 part white crème de cacao
1 part Bols® Lychee
Splash of grenadine
Shake with ice and strain into a cocktail glass.

PETTICOAT LANE

1 part Licor 43®
1 part Kahlua®
1 part cream
Shake with ice and strain into a cocktail glass.

PHEROMONE

2 parts cream
1 part dark rum
1 part peppermint schnapps
1 part brown crème de cacao
Splash of Bacardi 151®
Shake with ice and strain into a cocktail glass.

PHLEGM

2 parts dark rum
1 part crème de banana
1 part lime juice
Garnish: lemon wedge
Shake with ice and strain into a cocktail glass. Garnish
with lemon wedge.

PICCADILLY CIRCUS

1 part apricot brandy
1 part white wine
Splash of tonic water
Shake with ice and strain into a cocktail glass.

PICK ME UP

3 parts fernet
1 part pastis
Build on ice in a rocks glass and stir.

PICK OF THE LITTER

2 parts light rum
1 part dark rum
1 part peach schnapps
1 part orange juice
1 part pineapple juice
Shake with ice and strain into a cocktail glass.

PICKANINNY

2 parts watermelon liqueur
1 part vodka
1 part soda
Shake with ice and strain into a cocktail glass.

PIERRE COLLINS

3 parts sour mix
2 parts brandy
1 part soda
Garnish: orange slice and cherry
Build on ice in a tall glass and stir.
Garnish with orange slice and cherry.

PIKE'S PEAK

2 parts pineapple juice
2 parts apple juice
1 part scotch
1 part Amaretto
1 part coffee brandy
Build on ice in a tall glass and stir.

PIMP COCKTAIL

2 parts vodka
2 parts orange juice
1 part blue curaçao
1 part peach schnapps
Garnish: orange slice

Shake with ice and strain into a cocktail glass. Garnish
with orange slice.

PIÑA COLADA

2 parts cream of coconut
1 part light rum
1 part pineapple juice
Garnish: pineapple wedge and whipped cream

Mix with ice in a blender and pour into a glass. Garnish
with pineapple wedge and whipped cream.

PINEAPPLE RUM CASSIS

1 part light rum
1 part crème de cassis
1 part pineapple juice
Shake with ice and strain into a cocktail glass.

PINK CAD

2 parts tequila
1 part Pama®
1 part sour mix
Shake with ice and strain into a cocktail glass.

PINK CALIFORNIA SUNSHINE

3 parts rosé champagne
1 part crème de cassis
Pour into a champagne flute.

PINK ELEPHANTS ON PARADE

1 part vodka
1 part Midori®
1 part pink lemonade
Shake with ice and strain into a cocktail glass.

PINK FLUID

1 part vodka
1 part white crème de cacao
1 part sloe gin
Garnish: strawberry
Shake with ice and strain into a cocktail glass. Garnish
with strawberry.

PINK FOREST

2 parts Bols® Strawberry
1 part gin
1 part cream
Splash of triple sec
Stir with ice and strain into a cocktail glass.

PINK JESTER

1 part vanilla vodka
1 part root bear schnapps
Shake with ice and strain into a cocktail glass.

PINK SQUIRREL

2 parts cream
1 part white crème de cacao
1 part crème de noyaux
Shake with ice and strain into a cocktail glass.

PINK SURPRISE

2 parts lemonade
1 part cherry brandy
Dash of bitters
Shake with ice and strain into a cocktail glass.

PINK TRACY

2 parts vodka
1 part Malibu Coconut Rum®
1 part pineapple juice
Splash of grenadine
Shake with ice and strain into a cocktail glass.

PINKY-TINI

2 parts Absolut® Mandarin
1 part sloe gin
1 part white wine
Splash of triple sec
Garnish: orange twist
Shake with ice and strain into a double rocks glass.
Garnish with orange twist.

PISANG GARUDA

1 part Pisang Ambon®
1 part light rum
1 part cream
Shake with ice and strain into a cocktail glass.

PISANG PASSION

1 part vodka
1 part Pisang Ambon®
1 part Kahlua®
1 part cream
Shake with ice and strain into a cocktail glass.

PISCO KID

1 part light rum
1 part pisco
1 part pineapple juice
Shake with ice and strain into a cocktail glass.

PISCO SOUR

2 parts pisco
1 part lime juice
1 tablespoon syrup
1 egg white
Dash of bitters
Shake with ice and strain into a cocktail glass.

PISS IN THE SNOW

2 parts cream
1 part white crème de cacao
1 part white crème de menthe
1 part Galliano®
Shake cream, white crème de cacao, and white crème de
menthe with ice and strain into a
cocktail glass. Top with Galliano.

PISTOLERO

1 part Bols® Genever
Splash of Bols® Maraschino
Dash of dry vermouth
Shake with ice and strain into a cocktail glass.

PLANTER'S PUNCH

2 parts sour mix
2 parts orange juice
1 part light rum
1 part dark rum
1 part amber rum
1 part grenadine
Splash of soda
Dash of bitters
Garnish: orange slice and cherry
Build on ice in a tall glass and stir.
Garnish with orange slice and cherry.

PLAY DATE

1 part pomegranate vodka
1 part pineapple juice
1 part lemonade
Shake with ice and strain into a cocktail glass.

PLAY WITH FIRE

1 part brandy
Splash of chocolate liqueur
Splash of grenadine
Shake with ice and strain into a cocktail glass.

PLAY WITH ME

2 parts Mandarine Napoléon®
1 part tequila
1 part triple sec
Splash of lime juice (freshly squeezed)
Shake with ice and strain into a cocktail glass.

PLAYER'S PASSION

2 parts sparkling wine
1 part Alizé® Rose
1 part Cognac
Pour into a champagne flute.

PLAYING CATCH

2 parts gin
1 part Bols® Red Orange
Splash of lime juice
Dash of bitters
Stir with ice and strain into a cocktail glass.

PLAYMATE

1 part whiskey
1 egg white
Splash of sambuca
Shake with ice and strain into a cocktail glass.

PLEASURE SHIVER

2 parts strawberry milk
1 part vodka
1 part white crème de cacao
1 part Tia Maria®
Garnish: chocolate rim
Shake with ice and strain into a chocolate-rimmed
cocktail glass.

PLUTO

1 part white wine
1 part orange juice
Splash of apricot brandy
Pour into a wine glass and stir.

POINT OF NO RETURN

2 parts pineapple juice
1 part Bacardi® Gold Reserve
Splash of sloe gin
Splash of lime juice (freshly squeezed)
Shake with ice and strain into a cocktail glass.

POLISH SIDECAR

2 parts gin
1 part blackberry schnapps
Stir with ice and strain into a cocktail glass.

POLYNESIAN APPLE

2 parts apple brandy
1 part bourbon
1 part grapefruit juice
Shake with ice and strain into a cocktail glass.

POMEGRANATE MARTINI

3 parts Pama®
1 part vodka
Splash of cranberry juice
Splash of sour mix
Garnish: lemon twist
Shake with ice and strain into a cocktail glass. Garnish
with lemon twist.

POMEGRANATE SOUR

2 parts Pama®

1 part sour mix

Splash of soda

Shake with ice and strain into a cocktail glass.

POMEGRANATE SPRITZER

2 parts white wine

1 part pomegranate schnapps

1 part tonic water

Pour into a wine glass and stir.

POM-POM

2 parts Pama®

1 part vodka

1 part pineapple juice

Garnish: cherry

Shake with ice and strain into a cocktail glass. Garnish with cherry.

PONTBERRY MARTINI

2 parts pomegranate vodka

1 part blackberry schnapps

1 part grape juice

Shake with ice and strain into a cocktail glass.

POOP DECK COCKTAIL

1 part Cognac

1 part blackberry brandy

1 part white wine

Shake with ice and strain into a cocktail glass.

POPPIN' CHERRY

2 parts cherry cola

1 part cherry vodka

Splash of grenadine

Garnish: cherry

Build on ice in a highball glass.

Garnish with cherry.

POPULATION KILLER

2 parts pineapple juice

1 part Kirschwasser

1 part peppermint schnapps

1 egg white

Shake with ice and strain into a cocktail glass.

PORCH MONKEY

1 part grape vodka

1 part lemonade

Shake with ice and strain into a cocktail glass.

PORT WINE COBBLER

1 part triple sec

1 part port wine

Splash of grenadine

Shake with ice and strain into a cocktail glass.

POWER UP

2 parts crème de cassis
1 part vodka
1 part strawberry juice
1 part blackberry juice
Build on ice in a highball glass and stir.

PRAIRIE OYSTER

1 part Cognac
1 part tomato juice
Splash of hot sauce
Garnish: oyster
Build on ice in a highball glass and stir. Garnish with oyster.

PRANKSTER

1 part crème de banana
1 part triple sec
1 part sour mix
Shake with ice and strain into a cocktail glass.

PREAKNESS

1 part whiskey

Splash of Bénédictine

Dash of bitters

Dash of sweet vermouth

Shake with ice and strain into a cocktail glass.

PRELUDE TO A KISS

2 parts ginger ale

1 part gin

1 part peach schnapps

Splash of grenadine

Stir with ice and strain into a cocktail glass.

PRESBYTERIAN

1 part whiskey

1 part ginger ale

1 part tonic water

Build on ice in a highball glass.

PRETTY ANGEL

1 part crème de banana
1 part dark rum
1 part peppermint schnapps
1 part cream
Garnish: ground nutmeg
Shake with ice and strain into a cocktail glass. Garnish
with ground nutmeg.

PRETTY DELIGHTFUL

1 part peach schnapps
1 part sloe gin
1 part tonic water
Shake with ice and strain into a cocktail glass.

PRETTY THING

2 parts vodka
1 part coffee liqueur
1 part cream
Splash of crème de noyaux
Shake with ice and strain into a cocktail glass.

PRIMAVERA

2 parts Licor 43®
1 part Parfait Amour
Splash of grenadine
Garnish: cherry
Shake with ice and strain into a cocktail glass. Garnish
with cherry.

PRIMER

1 part peppermint schnapps
1 part peach schnapps
1 part cherry brandy
Shake with ice and strain into a cocktail glass.

PRINCE CHARLES

1 part gin
1 part port wine
Splash of lime juice
Stir with ice and strain into a cocktail glass.

PRINCESS GEORGIE GIRL

2 parts champagne
1 part blueberry vodka
1 part lemonade
Garnish: sugar rim and blueberries
Pour into a sugar-rimmed champagne flute. Garnish
with blueberries.

PROSPECTOR MARTINI

2 parts vanilla vodka
1 part cinnamon schnapps
1 part butterscotch schnapps
Shake with ice and strain into a cocktail glass.

PSYCHO

2 parts light rum
1 part orange juice
1 part pineapple juice
Splash of Galliano®
Splash of grenadine
Build on ice in a highball glass and stir.

PSYCHO CITRUS

3 parts orange juice
1 part strawberry vodka
1 part tequila
1 part white crème de menthe
1 part triple sec
Build on ice in a tall glass and stir.

PUCKER UP

1 part sloe gin
1 part crème de cassis
1 part cranberry juice
Splash of lime juice (freshly squeezed)
Shake with ice and strain into a cocktail glass.

PUCKERITA

1 part tequila
1 part apple schnapps
Splash of lime juice
Shake with ice and strain into a cocktail glass.

PUMA BLOOD

1 part gin
1 part coconut brandy
Splash of triple sec
Stir with ice and strain into a cocktail glass.

PUMPKIN EATER

1 part light rum
1 part triple sec
1 part orange juice
Splash of cream
Garnish: orange slice and cherry
Shake with ice and strain into a cocktail glass. Garnish
with orange slice and cherry.

PUMPKIN MARTINI

2 parts spiced rum
2 parts cola
1 part brown crème de cacao
Shake with ice and strain into a cocktail glass.

PUMPKIN PIE

1 part coffee liqueur
1 part Irish cream
Splash of cinnamon schnapps
Dash of Bacardi 151®
Shake with ice and strain into a cocktail glass.

PUNCHY

2 parts pineapple juice
1 part vodka
1 part crème de banana
1 part orange juice
Splash of grenadine
Garnish: orange slice
Build on ice in a tall glass and stir.
Garnish with orange slice.

PUPPET MASTER

2 parts coffee
1 part whiskey
1 part coffee brandy
Garnish: whipped cream
Pour into an Irish coffee glass and stir. Garnish with
whipped cream.

PURE JOY

1 part tequila
1 part crème de cassis
1 part peppermint schnapps
1 part lemon–lime soda
Shake with ice and strain into a cocktail glass.

PURPLE ALASKAN

2 parts orange juice
1 part whiskey
1 part Southern Comfort®
1 part Chambord®
Splash of Amaretto
Shake with ice and strain into a cocktail glass.

PURPLE CRAYON

2 parts Chambord®
2 parts pineapple juice
Splash of vodka
Shake with ice and strain into a cocktail glass.

PURPLE FLIRT

2 parts vodka
1 part black sambuca
Shake with ice and strain into a cocktail glass.

PURPLE HOOTER COCKTAIL

3 parts sour mix
1 part blueberry vodka
1 part raspberry liqueur
Build on ice in a highball glass and stir.

PURPLE KISS

2 parts gin
2 parts crème de noyaux
1 part lemon juice
Splash of cherry brandy
Stir with ice and strain into a cocktail glass.

PURPLE LOVE

2 parts blue curaçao
2 parts lemon-lime soda
1 part light rum
1 part Chambord®
Garnish: whipped cream
Shake with ice and strain into a cocktail glass. Garnish
with whipped cream.

PURPLE RAIN

3 parts sour mix
1 part tequila
1 part light rum
1 part vodka
1 part triple sec
1 part Chambord®
Build on ice in a tall glass and stir.

PURPLE RAIN COOLER

2 parts grape soda
1 part vodka
1 part Parfait Amour
Build on ice in a highball glass and stir.

PYT

2 parts champagne
1 part apricot brandy
1 part cranberry juice
Splash of lime juice
Pour into a champagne flute and stir

QUAKER'S COCKTAIL

1 part light rum
1 part brandy
1 part lemon juice
1 tablespoon of syrup
Garnish: lemon wedge
Shake with ice and strain into a cocktail glass.

QUAKING

1 part whiskey
1 part crème de cassis
1 part Amaretto
Splash of pineapple juice
Shake with ice and strain into a cocktail glass.

QUEEN BEE

1 part Absolut® Citron
1 part coffee brandy
1 part sherry
Shake with ice and strain into a cocktail glass.

QUEEN OF SCOTS

2 parts scotch
1 part Chartreuse
1 part lemon juice (freshly squeezed)
Pinch of sugar
Shake with ice and strain into a cocktail glass.

QUEEN'S LOVE

1 part advocaat
1 part cherry brandy
1 part grapefruit juice
Garnish: Cherry
Shake with ice and strain into a cocktail glass. Garnish
with cherry.

QUICK THRILL

1 part Bacardi® dark rum

1 part red wine

1 part cola

Shake Bacardi® dark rum and red wine with ice and
strain into a wine glass. Top with cola.

QUIET SUNDAY

1 part vodka

1 part orange juice

Splash of Amaretto

Splash of grenadine

Garnish: lemon slice

Shake with ice and strain into a cocktail glass. Garnish
with lemon slice.

RABBIT FOOD

3 parts light rum
1 part carrot juice
Splash of sour mix
Shake with ice and strain into a cocktail glass.

RACE TO THE FINISH

1 part vanilla vodka
Splash of tequila
Dash of dry vermouth
Shake with ice and strain into a cocktail glass.

RADICAL

1 part whiskey

1 part sake

1 part soda water

1 tablespoon of syrup

Shake with ice and strain into a cocktail glass.

RAFTER

2 parts Campari®

1 part gin

1 part lime cordial

Dash of dry vermouth

Stir with ice and strain into a cocktail glass.

RAGTIME

2 parts coffee

1 part Kahlua®

1 part brandy

1 part cream

Garnish: coffee beans

Pour into an Irish coffee glass and stir. Float coffee beans
on top.

RAHJOHANNA

2 parts Absolut® Citron

2 parts Pisang Ambon®

2 parts tonic water

1 part strawberry liqueur

1 egg white

Build on ice in a highball glass and stir.

RAINBOW

2 parts blue curaçao

1 part cherry brandy

1 part vodka

1 part ginger ale

Garnish: scoop of vanilla ice cream

Build on ice in a tall glass and stir.

Top with scoop of vanilla ice cream.

RAINFOREST

2 parts coconut cream

1 part gin

1 part blue curaçao

Garnish: pineapple wedge

Stir with ice and strain into a cocktail glass. Garnish
with pineapple wedge.

RAINFOREST CAFÉ

1 part raspberry vodka

1 part peach schnapps

Splash of lime juice (freshly squeezed)

Pinch of sugar

Garnish: lime wedge

Shake with ice and strain into a cocktail glass. Garnish
with lime wedge.

RARE TREAT

1 part vodka

1 part Parfait Amour

1 part cherry brandy

1 part cream

Shake with ice and strain into a cocktail glass.

RARIN' TO GO

2 parts dark rum
1 part peppermint schnapps
1 part cola
Garnish: mint sprig
Shake with ice and strain into a cocktail glass. Garnish
with mint sprig.

RASPBERRY LIME RICKEY

1 part raspberry vodka
1 part lemon-lime soda
Splash of lime juice (freshly squeezed)
Shake with ice and strain into a cocktail glass.

RASPBERRIES AND CREAM

2 parts cream
1 part white crème de cacao
1 part raspberry liqueur
Shake with ice and strain into a cocktail glass.

RASPBERRY BLUSH

1 part dark rum

1 part raspberry liqueur

Splash of lime juice

Dash of dry vermouth

Shake with ice and strain into a cocktail glass.

RASPBERRY KAMIKAZE

2 parts vodka

2 parts sour mix

1 part Chambord®

Shake with ice and strain into a cocktail glass.

RASPBERRY LEMONADE

2 parts sparkling wine

1 part raspberry liqueur

1 part lemonade

Pour into a wine glass and stir.

RASPBERRY PASSION

2 parts vodka

1 part raspberry liqueur

1 part passion fruit juice

Shake with ice and strain into a cocktail glass.

RASPBERRY PUNCH

2 parts fruit punch

1 part raspberry vodka

Dash of bitters

Shake with ice and strain into a cocktail glass.

RASPBERRY SOUR

2 parts sour mix

1 part Chambord®

Garnish: orange slice and cherry

Shake with ice and strain into a rocks glass. Garnish
with orange slice and cherry.

RASPBERRY STUPID

2 parts lemon-lime soda
1 part gin
1 part raspberry liqueur
Stir with ice and strain into a cocktail glass.

RATTLESNAKE

1 part scotch
1 part Pisang Ambon®
Splash of pineapple juice
Shake with ice and strain into a cocktail glass.

RATTLESNAKE COCKTAIL

1 part whiskey
1 part anisette
Splash of lime juice
Pinch of sugar
1 egg white
Shake with ice and strain into a cocktail glass.

RAZZ REVENGE

2 parts Amaretto
2 parts light rum
1 part raspberry lemonade
Shake with ice and strain into a cocktail glass.

RAZZMOPOLITAN

3 parts vodka
1 part raspberry liqueur
Splash of lime juice (freshly squeezed)
Shake with ice and strain into a cocktail glass.

READY OR NOT

2 parts white grape juice
1 part vodka
1 part blue curaçao
Shake with ice and strain into a cocktail glass.

REALITY BITES

1 part vodka
1 part peppermint schnapps
1 part pineapple juice
Garnish: pineapple wedge
Shake with ice and strain into a cocktail glass. Garnish
with pineapple slice.

REALLY GREAT

1 part rum
1 part cherry schnapps
1 part cola
Garnish: cherry
Shake with ice and strain into a cocktail glass. Garnish
with cherry.

REBEL RAIDER

2 parts lemonade
1 part bourbon
1 part Mandarine Napoléon®
Splash of sherry
Splash of tonic water
Build on ice in a highball glass and stir.

RECESSION PROOF

2 parts Absolut® Citron
1 part triple sec
Splash of cranberry juice
Splash of lime juice
Shake with ice and strain into a cocktail glass.

RED ALERT

2 parts sour mix
1 part tequila
1 part crème de banana
1 part sloe gin
Build on ice in a highball glass and stir.

RED APPLE

1 part vodka
1 part apple juice
Splash of grenadine
Splash of lime juice
Shake with ice and strain into a cocktail glass.

RED BALL

1 part tonic water
1 part iced tea
1 part light rum
Splash of Passoã®
Splash of lime juice (freshly squeezed)
Build on ice in a highball glass and stir.

RED BARON

1 part sloe gin
1 part lemonade
Garnish: cherry
Shake with ice and strain into a cocktail glass.

RED CLOUD

2 parts gin
1 part coconut brandy
Splash of grenadine
Splash of lime juice
Stir with ice and strain into a cocktail glass.

RED DEVIL

4 parts orange juice
1 part vodka
1 part triple sec
1 part Southern Comfort®
1 part sloe gin
1 part Amaretto
1 part soda
Garnish: orange slice and cherry
Build on ice in a tall glass and stir.
Garnish with orange slice and cherry.

RED DEVIL REVIVER

1 part whiskey
1 part tomato juice
Splash of Worcestershire sauce
Dash of pepper
Build on ice in a highball glass and stir.

RED DOG MARTINI

1 part vodka
1 part port wine
Splash of grenadine
Shake with ice and strain into a cocktail glass.

RED HOT PASSION

1 part bourbon
1 part Amaretto
1 part Southern Comfort®
1 part pineapple juice
1 part orange juice
1 part cranberry juice
Build on ice in a tall glass and stir.

RED LEMONADE

1 part red wine
1 part triple sec
1 part lemonade
Pour into a wine glass and stir.

RED PANTIES

2 parts orange juice
1 part vodka
1 part peach schnapps
Splash of grenadine
Shake with ice and strain into a cocktail glass.

RED PASSION MARTINI

1 part Passoã®
1 part pineapple juice
Splash of Campari®
Shake with ice and strain into a cocktail glass.

RED ROCKER

1 part chocolate vodka
Dash of grenadine
Garnish: strawberry syrup rim
Shake with ice and strain into a strawberry-syrup
rimmed cocktail glass.

RED RUSSIAN

1 part vodka
1 part white crème de cacao
1 part cranberry juice
Shake with ice and strain into a cocktail glass.

RED SKY

1 part Bacardi® Limon
Splash of crème de cassis
Splash of crème de violette
Shake with ice and strain into a cocktail glass.

RED SNAPPER

3 parts cranberry juice

1 part whiskey

1 part Amaretto

1 part soda

Garnish: orange slice and cherry

Build on ice in a tall glass and stir. Garnish with orange slice and cherry.

RED WINE COBBLER

2 parts red wine

1 part orange juice

Splash of lime juice

Garnish: cherry

Shake with ice and strain into a wine glass. Garnish with cherry.

RED, WHITE, AND BLUE

1 part gin

1 part Bols® Maraschino

1 part blue curaçao

Splash of lemon–lime soda

Shake with ice and strain into a cocktail glass.

RED-HEADED SLUT COCKTAIL

3 parts pineapple juice

2 parts peach schnapps

1 part Jägermeister®

Shake with ice and strain into a cocktail glass.

REFORM COCKTAIL

2 parts sherry

Dash of dry vermouth

Dash of bitters

Garnish: cherry

Shake with ice and strain into a cocktail glass. Garnish with cherry.

REFORMATION

2 parts Parfait Amour
1 part scotch
1 part cherry brandy
Shake with ice and strain into a cocktail glass.

RELAX

2 parts vodka
1 part pomegranate schnapps
1 part lemon–lime soda
Shake with ice and strain into a cocktail glass.

RENAISSANCE COCKTAIL

2 parts gin
1 part butterscotch schnapps
1 part cream
Garnish: ground nutmeg
Shake with ice and strain into a cocktail glass. Garnish
with ground nutmeg.

REPAIR KIT

2 parts anisette
1 part brandy
1 part white crème de cacao
Shake with ice and strain into a cocktail glass.

REPTILE

1 part whiskey
1 part orange juice
1 part ginger ale
Shake with ice and strain into a cocktail glass.

RESIDENCE

2 parts lemon-lime soda
1 part grape vodka
Splash of triple sec
Build on ice in a highball glass and stir.

REVOLUTION

1 part strawberry liqueur
1 part Mandarine Napoléon®
1 part cranberry juice
Shake with ice and strain into a cocktail glass.

RHETT BUTLER

2 parts Southern Comfort®
1 part lemon-lime soda
Splash of lime juice (freshly squeezed)
Shake with ice and strain into a cocktail glass.

RICHELIEU

1 part bourbon
1 part Licor 43®
Splash of cream
Shake with ice and strain into a cocktail glass.

RINGO

2 parts cola

1 part sloe gin

1 part Malibu Coconut Rum®

1 part brandy

Splash of grenadine

Build on ice in a highball glass and stir.

RIO BLANCO

1 part dark rum

Splash of brown crème de cacao

Splash of blue curaçao

Garnish: lemon wedge

Shake with ice and strain into a cocktail glass. Garnish with lemon wedge.

RIO SPARKLER

2 parts cachaça

1 part sparkling wine

1 part pear brandy

1 part pomegranate juice

Pinch of brown sugar

Build on ice in a highball glass and stir.

RIP THE SHEETS ORGASM

1 part vodka

1 part hazelnut liqueur

1 part Bols® Vanilla

Garnish: scoop of vanilla ice cream

Build on ice in a highball glass and stir. Top with scoop
of vanilla ice cream.

RIPE MARSHMALLOW

2 parts cherry brandy

1 part white crème de cacao

1 part cream

Shake with ice and strain into a cocktail glass.

RISKY BUSINESS

1 part apricot brandy

1 part Kirschwasser

Splash of dry vermouth

Shake with ice and strain into a cocktail glass.

ROAD RUNNER

1 part Tia Maria®

1 part Grand Marnier®

Shake with ice and strain into a cocktail glass.

ROB ROY

1 part scotch
Dash of sweet vermouth
Garnish: cherry
Shake with ice and strain into a cocktail glass. Garnish
with cherry.

ROBBER BARON

3 parts vodka
1 part cherry brandy
Dash of dry vermouth
Garnish: cherry
Shake with ice and strain into a cocktail glass. Garnish
with cherry.

ROBIN'S NEST

2 parts cherry vodka
1 part white crème de cacao
1 part cranberry juice
Shake with ice and strain into a cocktail glass.

ROCK MY WORLD

2 parts pineapple juice
1 part cranberry juice
1 part rum
1 part melon liqueur
1 part Bols® Coconut
Build on ice in a highball glass and stir.

ROCK OUT

2 parts Jim Beam®
1 part orange juice
Shake with ice and strain into a cocktail glass.

ROCK THROWER

1 part tequila
1 part fernet
Splash of anisette
Shake with ice and strain into a cocktail glass.

ROCOCO

1 part grape vodka

1 part triple sec

1 part cola

Shake with ice and strain into a cocktail glass.

ROLLER COASTER

3 parts lemonade

1 part gin

1 part brandy

1 part peppermint schnapps

Build on ice in a highball glass and stir.

ROLLING HOME

2 parts light rum

1 part Pisang Ambon®

1 part cream

Shake with ice and strain into a cocktail glass.

ROLLING THUNDER

1 part light rum
1 part apple schnapps
Splash of lime juice
Splash of grenadine
Splash of soda
Shake with ice and strain into a cocktail glass.

ROLLS ROYCE

1 part gin
1 part Dubonnet blonde
Splash of anisette
Dash of dry vermouth
Stir with ice and strain into a cocktail glass.

ROLY-POLY

1 part peach schnapps
1 part blue curaçao
1 part pineapple juice
Shake with ice and strain into a cocktail glass.

ROMAN SNOWBALL

1 part sambuca
1 part Bailey's Irish Cream®
1 part coffee liqueur
Splash of cream
Shake with ice and strain into a cocktail glass.

ROMAN STINGER

2 parts brandy
1 part white crème de menthe
1 part sambuca
Shake with ice and strain into a cocktail glass.

ROMANCE COCKTAIL

2 parts brandy
1 part Pama®
Splash of sweet vermouth
Shake with ice and strain into a cocktail glass.

ROMANTIC DREAM

1 part Malibu Coconut Rum®
1 part Pisang Ambon®
1 part pineapple juice
1 part orange juice
Build on ice in a highball glass and stir.

ROOT BEER FLOAT

1 part Kahlua®
1 part root beer schnapps
1 part cola
Splash of Galliano®
Shake Kahlua®, root beer schnapps, and cola
with ice and strain into a cocktail glass.
Top with Galliano®.

ROOT OF THINGS

2 parts Bailey's Irish Cream®
1 part root beer schnapps
1 part cinnamon schnapps
1 part cream
Shake with ice and strain into a cocktail glass.

ROSE LEMONADE

2 parts rosé wine
1 part strawberry liqueur
1 part pink lemonade
Garnish: strawberry
Pour into a wine glass and stir.
Garnish with strawberry.

ROSE-COLORED GLASS

2 parts vodka
1 part strawberry liqueur
1 part pink lemonade
Garnish: lemon wedge

Shake with ice and strain into a cocktail glass. Garnish
with lemon wedge.

ROTTEN ORANGE

2 parts sour mix
1 part Grand Marnier®

Shake with ice and strain into a cocktail glass.

ROUGE MARTINI

1 part gin
Splash of Chambord®

Stir with ice and strain into a cocktail glass.

ROUGE SPECIAL

2 parts pastis

1 part brandy

1 part lemonade

Splash of grenadine

Shake with ice and strain into a cocktail glass.

ROYAL EXOTIC

2 parts pineapple juice

1 part apricot brandy

1 part pastis

Splash of grenadine

Shake with ice and strain into a cocktail glass.

ROYAL MANDARINE

2 parts orange juice

1 part Mandarine Napoléon®

1 part white crème de cacao

Shake with ice and strain into a cocktail glass.

ROYAL PALACE

2 parts vodka
1 part Amaretto
1 part peach juice
Splash of peach schnapps
Shake with ice and strain into a cocktail glass.

ROYAL ROOST

2 parts bourbon
1 part pastis
1 part tripe sec
Dash of bitters
Garnish: orange slice
Shake with ice and strain into a cocktail glass. Garnish
with orange slice.

ROYAL TEMPTATION

2 parts Amaretto
2 parts cream
1 part melon liqueur
Shake with ice and strain into a cocktail glass.

RUBY RED

2 parts gin
1 part cherry brandy
1 part pomegranate schnapps
Dash of dry vermouth
Stir with ice and strain into a cocktail glass.

RUDE COSMOPOLITAN

3 parts tequila
1 part blue curaçao
Splash of lime juice
Dash of bitters
Shake with ice and strain into a cocktail glass.

RULE MY WORLD

2 parts orange juice
1 part rum
1 part Amaretto
1 part pineapple juice
1 part strawberry liqueur
Build on ice in a highball glass and stir.

RUM AID

1 part Malibu Coconut Rum®

1 part spiced rum

1 part triple sec

1 part sour mix

1 part ginger ale

1 part cranberry juice

Splash of Bacardi 151®

Build on ice in a tall glass and stir.

RUM DE MENTHE

2 parts dark rum

1 part white crème de menthe

1 part cola

Build on ice in a tall glass and stir.

RUM DUBONNET

1 part light rum

1 part Dubonnet blonde

1 part lemonade

Garnish: lemon wedge

Shake with ice and strain into a cocktail glass. Garnish with lemon wedge.

RUM REFRESHER

2 parts light rum

1 part lime juice

Pinch of sugar

Garnish: basil leaves

Shake with ice and strain into a cocktail glass. Garnish with basil leaves.

RUM RUMMY

2 parts light rum
1 part orange juice
1 tablespoon of syrup
Splash of lime juice (freshly squeezed)
Dash of bitters
Shake with ice and strain into a cocktail glass.

RUM RUNNER

2 parts orange juice
2 parts pineapple juice
1 part light rum
1 part blackberry brandy
1 part crème de banana
1 part grenadine
Splash of Bacardi 151®
Garnish: pineapple wedge
Build on ice in a tall glass and stir. Top with Bacardi
151®. Garnish with pineapple wedge.

RUM SALAD

2 parts light rum
1 part triple sec
1 part soda
Garnish: chopped cucumber and mint sprig
Shake with ice and strain into a cocktail glass. Garnish
with chopped cucumber and mint sprig.

RUM SOUR

2 parts sour mix
1 part light rum
Garnish: orange slice and cherry
Shake with ice and strain into a rocks glass. Garnish
with orange slice and cherry.

RUM SPICE WHACKER

1 part spiced rum
1 part coffee liqueur
1 part Dumante®
1 part cream
Shake with ice and strain into a cocktail glass.

RUM SWIRL

1 part light rum
1 part crème de banana
1 part Dumante®
Shake with ice and strain into a cocktail glass.

RUM'N RAISIN

2 parts dark rum
2 parts cream
1 part Bols® Chocolate Mint
Garnish: scoop of rum raisin ice cream
and chocolate syrup
Build on ice in a highball glass and stir.
Top with scoop of rum raisin ice cream
and chocolate syrup.

RUMBA

1 part dark rum
1 part brown crème de cacao
Splash of pineapple juice
Splash of grenadine
Shake with ice and strain into a rocks glass.

RUSHIN' AROUND

2 parts vodka
1 part Tia Maria®
1 part cinnamon schnapps
Garnish: cinnamon powder
Shake with ice and strain into a cocktail glass. Dust with
cinnamon powder.

RUSHING

1 part bourbon
1 part Bailey's Irish Cream®
1 part Amaretto
1 part cola
Shake with ice and strain into a rocks glass.

RUSSIAN APPLE

2 parts vodka

1 part apple schnapps

1 part pineapple juice

Shake with ice and strain into a cocktail glass.

RUSSIAN BEAR COCKTAIL

2 parts vodka

2 parts coconut cream

1 part root beer schnapps

1 part butterscotch schnapps

Shake with ice and strain into a cocktail glass.

RUSSIAN GOLD

3 parts vodka

1 part Galliano®

1 part crème de banana

1 part orange juice

Shake with ice and strain into a cocktail glass.

RUSSIAN HAZE

2 parts vodka
1 part Frangelico®
1 part Bailey's Irish Cream® Mint Chocolate
Garnish: chocolate syrup rim
Shake with ice and strain into a chocolate-rimmed
cocktail glass.

RUSSIAN JACK

2 parts sour mix
1 part Jack Daniel's®
1 part vodka
Shake with ice and strain into a cocktail glass.

RUSSIAN NUT

1 part vodka
1 part crème de noyaux
Dash of bitters
Shake with ice and strain into a rocks glass.

RUSSIAN SUNTAN

3 parts apple cider
3 parts pineapple juice
1 part gin
1 part rum
1 part vodka
Build on ice in a tall glass and stir.

RUSSIAN TURBULENCE

1 part vodka
1 part Red Bull®
Build on ice in a highball glass.

RUSTY NAIL

3 parts scotch
1 part Drambuie®
Build on ice in a rocks glass.

RYE AND DRY

2 parts whiskey

1 part ginger ale

Dash of dry vermouth

Shake with ice and strain into a cocktail glass.

SAGA SPECIAL

1 part vodka

1 part coffee liqueur

1 part triple sec

1 part lemonade

Shake with ice and strain into a cocktail glass.

SAIL AWAY

2 parts orange vodka

1 part Midori®

1 part lemon-lime soda

Shake with ice and strain into a cocktail glass.

SAINT BERNARD

1 part apricot brandy
1 part port wine
Splash of lime juice
Splash of tonic water
Shake with ice and strain into a cocktail glass.

SAINT MISBEHAVIN'

2 parts sparkling wine
1 part vanilla vodka
1 part strawberry liqueur
Pour into a wine glass and stir.

SAKE COCKTAIL

1 part Absolut® Citron
1 part melon liqueur
1 part sake
Shake with ice and strain into a cocktail glass.

SAKETINI

3 parts gin
1 part sake
Garnish: olive

Stir with ice and strain into a cocktail glass. Garnish with olive.

SALEM WITCH

2 parts sour mix
1 part tonic water
1 part vodka
1 part raspberry liqueur
1 part Midori®
Splash of grenadine

Build on ice in a tall glass and stir.

SALT AND PEPPER MARTINI

2 parts spiced rum

1 part ginger ale

1 part lemonade

1 tablespoon of syrup

Shake with ice and strain into a cocktail glass.

SALTY DOG

2 parts grapefruit juice

1 part vodka

Garnish: salt rim

Build on ice in a salt-rimmed highball glass.

SALUTE

1 part gin

1 part crème de cassis

1 part sweet vermouth

Splash of tonic water

Stir with ice and strain into a cocktail glass.

SAM FROM MEXICO

2 parts sambuca
1 part tequila
1 part grenadine
Splash of pineapple juice
Shake with ice and strain into a cocktail glass.

SAMBA

2 parts Goldschläger®
2 parts pineapple juice
1 part vodka
Shake with ice and strain into a cocktail glass.

SAMBA CINNAMON

3 parts cinnamon schnapps
2 parts cream
1 part sambuca
Splash of pineapple juice
Shake with ice and strain into a cocktail glass.

SAMBUCA BLITZ

1 part crème de cassis
1 part sambuca
Splash of tonic water
Dash of dry vermouth
Shake with ice and strain into a cocktail glass.

SAMBUCATINI

1 part vodka
Splash of blue curaçao
Splash of black sambuca
Shake with ice and strain into a cocktail glass.

SAMURAI

3 parts sake
1 part triple sec
Splash of sour mix
Splash of lime juice (freshly squeezed)
Shake with ice and strain into a cocktail glass.

SAN FRANCISCO COCKTAIL

1 part gin
1 part sloe gin
Dash of sweet vermouth
Dash of dry vermouth
Dash of bitters
Garnish: cherry

Shake with ice and strain into a cocktail glass. Garnish with cherry.

SAN JUAN TEA

3 parts sour mix
1 part Bacardi® Limon
Splash of Bacardi 151®

Pour sour mix and Bacardi® Limon into a highball glass and stir. Top with Bacardi 151®.

SAN MARINO

1 part dark rum
1 part Bols® Blue
1 part grapefruit juice
Shake with ice and strain into a cocktail glass.

SANDPIPER

2 parts grapefruit juice
1 part light rum
1 part cherry brandy
Shake with ice and strain into a cocktail glass.

SANDY COLLINS

3 parts sour mix
2 parts scotch
1 part soda
Garnish: orange slice and cherry
Build on ice in a tall glass and stir. Garnish with orange
slice and cherry.

SANGRIA COCKTAIL

2 parts red wine

1 part pomegranate schnapps

Splash of triple sec

Garnish: cinnamon sticks

Pour into a wine glass and stir. Garnish with cinnamon
sticks.

SANTA CLAUS

3 parts vodka

1 part Amaretto

1 part grenadine

Shake with ice and strain into a cocktail glass.

SANTA FE

2 parts rosé wine

1 part soda

Splash of lime juice

Pour into a wine glass and stir.

SANTA MONICA PIER

3 parts Southern Comfort®
1 part triple sec
1 part cranberry juice
Shake with ice and strain into a cocktail glass.

SANTIAGO

2 parts light rum
1 part advocaat
1 part cream
Garnish: ground nutmeg
Shake with ice and strain into a cocktail glass. Garnish
with ground nutmeg.

SANTO DOMINGO

2 parts dark rum
2 parts Amaretto
1 part Dumante®
1 part cream
Shake with ice and strain into a cocktail glass.

SARATOGA

3 parts brandy
1 part cherry schnapps
Dash of bitters
Shake with ice and strain into a cocktail glass.

SATIN

2 parts cream
1 part blackberry schnapps
1 part strawberry liqueur
Shake with ice and strain into a cocktail glass.

SATIN ANGEL

2 parts vodka
1 part guava juice
Pinch of sugar
Shake with ice and strain into a cocktail glass.

SATIN DOLL

2 parts Armagnac
1 part triple sec
Splash of pineapple juice
Shake with ice and strain into a cocktail glass.

SATIN LADY

2 parts sparkling wine
1 part ginger ale
1 part Mandarine Napoléon®
Splash of grenadine
Pour into a wine glass and stir.

SAUCY SUE

1 part dark rum
1 part apricot brandy
1 part apple brandy
1 part lemon–lime soda
Shake with ice and strain into a cocktail glass.

SAVE ME

1 part pisco
1 part vodka
1 part raspberry liqueur
1 part lemon–lime soda
Shake with ice and strain into a cocktail glass.

SAVE THE PLANET

1 part vodka
1 part melon liqueur
1 part lemon–lime soda
Splash of Chartreuse
Shake with ice and strain into a cocktail glass.

SAVOY TANGO

2 parts cranberry juice
1 part apple brandy
1 part sloe gin
Garnish: lime wedge
Shake with ice and strain into a cocktail glass. Garnish
with lime wedge.

SAXOMAPHONE

1 part gin
1 part triple sec
1 part white crème de menthe
1 part orange juice
Shake with ice and strain into a cocktail glass.

SAYONARA

3 parts gin
2 parts sake
1 part triple sec
Stir with ice and strain into a cocktail glass.

SCANDAL

2 parts Irish Mist[®]
1 part blue curaçao
Splash of lime juice
Shake with ice and strain into a cocktail glass.

SCARLET COLADA

1 part light rum
1 part pineapple juice
1 part coconut brandy
Splash of triple sec
Shake with ice and strain into a cocktail glass.

SCARLET CRUSHER

2 parts mango juice
1 part tequila
1 part vodka
Splash of grenadine
Shake with ice and strain into a cocktail glass.

SCARLET LADY

1 part Campari®
1 part Mandarine Napoléon®
Splash of grenadine
Shake with ice and strain into a cocktail glass.

SCARLET O'HARA

2 parts cranberry juice
1 part Southern Comfort®
Garnish: lime wedge
Build on ice in a highball glass. Garnish with lime
wedge.

SCHEHERAZADE

2 parts gin
1 part rosé wine
1 part brandy
Splash of orange juice
Stir with ice and strain into a wine glass.

SCHVITZER

2 parts orange juice
1 part anisette
Splash of triple sec
Shake with ice and strain into a cocktail glass.

SCOOTER

1 part cherry brandy

1 part Amaretto

1 part cream

Garnish: cherry

Shake with ice and strain into a cocktail glass. Garnish with cherry.

SCOPE

1 part green crème de menthe

1 part ginger ale

Shake with ice and strain into a cocktail glass.

SCORPION'S STING

2 parts cola

1 part vanilla vodka

1 part chocolate vodka

Splash of peppermint schnapps

Shake with ice and strain into a cocktail glass.

SCOTCH BISHOP

3 parts scotch

1 part blue curaçao

Splash of lime juice

Dash of dry vermouth

Shake with ice and strain into a cocktail glass.

SCOTCH CITRUS

2 parts scotch

1 part Grand Marnier®

1 part lemon juice

Splash of grenadine

Shake scotch, Grand Marnier®, and lemon juice with
ice and strain into a cocktail glass.

Top with grenadine.

SCOTCH EXPLORER

2 parts scotch

1 part Amaretto

1 part sherry

Garnish: lemon slice

Shake with ice and strain into a cocktail glass. Garnish
with lemon slice.

SCOTCH FANTASY

3 parts scotch

1 part crème de banana

1 part crème de noyaux

Shake with ice and strain into a cocktail glass.

SCOTCH LEMONADE

2 parts lemonade

1 part scotch

1 part cranberry juice

Splash of apple brandy

Build on ice in a highball glass and stir.

SCOTCH MARTINI

4 parts scotch
1 part soda
Dash of sweet vermouth
Dash of bitters
Shake with ice and strain into a cocktail glass.

SCOTCH PEPPERMINT

1 part scotch
1 part white crème de cacao
1 part peppermint schnapps
1 tablespoon sugar
Garnish: mint sprig
Shake with ice and strain into a cocktail glass. Garnish
with mint sprig.

SCOTTISH MONKEY

2 parts scotch
1 part cola
Splash of crème de banana
Shake with ice and strain into a cocktail glass.

SCOTTISH PICK ME UP

1 part scotch
1 part coffee liqueur
1 part soda
Shake with ice and strain into a cocktail glass.

SCOTTISH PISS

1 part scotch
Splash of Amaretto
Splash of orange juice
Shake with ice and strain into a cocktail glass.

SCOTTISH RUNNER

1 part scotch
1 part light rum
Splash of anisette
Splash of lemon juice
Dash of bitters
Garnish: cherry
Shake with ice and strain into a cocktail glass. Garnish
with cherry.

SCREAMING BANANA BANSHEE

1 part blueberry vodka

1 part banana liqueur

1 part white crème de cacao

1 part cream

Shake with ice and strain into a cocktail glass.

SCREAMING CREAM SPECIAL

2 parts Bailey's Irish Cream®

1 part vodka

2 scoops of chocolate ice cream

Mix with ice in a blender and pour into a
highball glass.

SCREAMING GEORGIA BUTTER

2 parts vodka

1 part peach schnapps

1 part butterscotch schnapps

Splash of pineapple juice

Shake with ice and strain into a cocktail glass.

SCREAMING VIKING

3 parts grape vodka
1 part lime juice
Dash of dry vermouth
Shake with ice and strain into a cocktail glass.

SCREW ME

2 parts vodka
1 part Bols® Chocolate Mint
1 part tonic water
Shake with ice and strain into a cocktail glass.

SCREWDRIVER

2 parts orange juice
1 part vodka
Build on ice in a highball glass.

SCREWED

2 parts Yukon Jack®
1 part peach schnapps
1 part tonic water
Shake with ice and strain into a cocktail glass.

SEA BLUE MARTINI

2 parts gin
1 part Bols® Blue
Splash of blue curaçao
Stir with ice and strain into a cocktail glass.

SEA BREEZE

1 part vodka
1 part cranberry juice
1 part grapefruit juice
Build on ice in a highball glass.

SEA SIREN

2 parts light rum
1 part pineapple juice
1 part guava juice
Splash of grenadine
Shake with ice and strain into a rocks glass half filled
with ice.

SEAWEED

2 parts Finlandia® Arctic Pineapple
1 part melon liqueur
Splash of strawberry liqueur
Splash of pineapple juice
Shake with ice and strain into a cocktail glass.

SECRET MARTINI

2 parts Lillet
1 part strawberry liqueur
1 part tonic water
Shake with ice and strain into a cocktail glass.

SEDUCTION

2 parts orange juice
1 part light rum
1 part melon liqueur
Shake with ice and strain into a cocktail glass.

SEE YA LATER

3 parts lemonade
1 part vodka
1 part apricot brandy
1 part triple sec
Dash of sweet vermouth
Build on ice in a highball glass and stir.

SEEK AND FIND

2 parts pineapple juice
1 part sloe gin
1 part white crème de cacao
Shake with ice and strain into a cocktail glass.

SEETHER

3 parts vodka

2 parts orange juice

1 part cherry brandy

Dash of bitters

Shake with ice and strain into a cocktail glass.

SELF STARTER

2 parts gin

1 part sweet vermouth

1 part pastis

Stir with ice and strain into a cocktail glass.

SEÑOR FROG

2 parts apple juice

1 part melon liqueur

1 part raspberry liqueur

Shake with ice and strain into a cocktail glass.

SEÑOR JACQUES

2 parts Jose Cuervo®
1 part sweet vermouth
Dash of dry vermouth
Garnish: cherry
Shake with ice and strain into a cocktail glass. Garnish
with cherry.

SENSATION COCKTAIL

2 parts cranberry juice
1 part Drambuie®
Shake with ice and strain into a cocktail glass.

SERENADE

2 parts pineapple juice
1 part vodka
1 part Amaretto
1 part coconut brandy
Garnish: cherry
Shake with ice and strain into a cocktail glass. Garnish
with cherry.

SERENADE IN BLUE

1 part blueberry vodka

Splash of triple sec

Splash of lime juice (freshly squeezed)

Shake with ice and strain into a cocktail glass.

SERPENTINE

1 part Southern Comfort®

1 part brandy

1 part orange juice

Shake with ice and strain into a cocktail glass.

SET THE JUICE LOOSE

2 parts pineapple juice

1 part orange juice

1 part crème de banana

1 part apricot brandy

1 part cherry brandy

Build on ice in a tall glass and stir.

SEVEN WINS

2 parts gin
1 part grapefruit juice
1 part maraschino liqueur
Splash of soda
Stir with ice and strain into a cocktail glass.

SEVENTH HEAVEN COCKTAIL

2 parts gin
1 part Rumple Minze®
1 part grapefruit juice
Garnish: mint sprig
Stir with ice and strain into a cocktail glass. Garnish
with mint sprig.

SEVILLE COCKTAIL

2 parts gin
1 part sparkling wine
1 part orange juice
1 tablespoon of syrup
Stir with ice and strain into a cocktail glass.

SEWAGE SWEET

1 part créme de banana
1 part orange juice
1 part cola
Splash of triple sec
Shake with ice and strain into a cocktail glass.

SEX APPEAL

2 parts sour mix
1 part light rum
1 part Malibu Coconut Rum®
1 part melon liqueur
Splash of peach schnapps
Garnish: lemon twist
Build on ice in a highball glass and stir.
Garnish with lemon twist.

SEX IN GREECE

2 parts pineapple juice
2 parts orange juice
1 part peach schnapps
1 part Apfelkorn
Build on ice in a highball glass and stir.

SEX ON FIRE

1 part dark rum
1 part coffee brandy
1 part Lillet
Shake with ice and strain into a cocktail glass.

SEX ON THE BEACH

2 parts orange juice
2 parts cranberry juice
1 part vodka
1 part peach schnapps
Garnish: orange slice and cherry
Build on ice in a tall glass and stir. Garnish with orange
slice and cherry.

SEX ON THE KITCHEN FLOOR

1 part vodka
1 part peach schnapps
1 part melon liqueur
Splash of orange juice
Garnish: lemon wedge
Shake with ice and strain into a cocktail glass. Garnish
with lemon wedge.

SEX UNDER THE SUN

2 parts vodka

1 part sweet vermouth

1 part coffee liqueur

1 part pear juice

Dash of bitters

Shake with ice and strain into a cocktail glass.

SEX WITH THE TEACHER

2 parts banana juice

1 part Cognac

1 part Kirschwasser

Stir with ice and strain into a cocktail glass.

SEXUAL ASSAULT

1 part peppermint schnapps

1 part Bols® Maraschino

Splash of brandy

Splash of pineapple juice

Stir with ice and strain into a cocktail glass.

SEXY DEVIL

2 parts vodka
1 part Absolut® Kurant
Dash of dry vermouth
Shake with ice and strain into a cocktail glass.

SHAG IN THE SAND

4 parts orange juice
1 part Southern Comfort®
1 part sloe gin
1 part vodka
Splash of grenadine
Build on ice in a highball glass and stir.

SHAKE HANDS

2 parts cinnamon schnapps
2 parts tonic water
1 part vodka
Splash of grenadine
Shake with ice and strain into a cocktail glass.

SHAKE IT

2 parts tequila
2 parts grapefruit juice
1 part lemon juice
Splash of grenadine
Shake with ice and strain into a cocktail glass.

SHAMON

1 part peppermint schnapps
1 part Cognac
Garnish: mint sprig
Shake with ice and strain into a cocktail glass. Garnish
with mint sprig.

SHAMROCK

1 part whiskey
Splash of green crème de menthe
Dash of dry vermouth
Garnish: olive
Shake with ice and strain into a cocktail glass. Garnish
with olive.

SHANGHAI COCKTAIL

1 part light rum
1 part anisette
1 part sake
Splash of grenadine
Splash of lemon juice
Shake with ice and strain into a cocktail glass.

SHAPE SHIFTER

1 part bourbon
1 part peppermint schnapps
1 part lemon–lime soda
Splash of lime juice
Dash of bitters
Shake with ice and strain into a cocktail glass.

SHARK ATTACK

2 parts Voyant Chai Cream®
2 parts cream
Splash of vodka
Shake with ice and strain into a cocktail glass.

SHARK'S BREATH

1 part vodka
1 part light rum
1 part cranberry juice
1 part orange juice
Splash of lime juice (freshly squeezed)
Shake with ice and strain into a cocktail glass.

SHARK'S MAI TAI

2 parts sour mix
1 part dark rum
1 part light rum
Splash of grenadine
Dash of Bacardi 151®
Shake sour mix, dark rum, light rum, and grenadine
with ice and strain into a cocktail glass. Top with
Bacardi 151®.

SHARK BITE

2 parts orange juice
1 part dark rum
Splash of grenadine
Pour orange juice and dark rum into a highball glass
and stir. Top with grenadine.

SHARONA

1 part Dubonnet blonde
1 part orange juice
Dash of dry vermouth
Shake with ice and strain into a cocktail glass.

SHEER ELEGANCE

2 parts Amaretto
2 parts crème de cassis
1 part vodka
Shake with ice and strain into a cocktail glass.

SHERRY COBBLER

2 parts sherry

1 part Cognac

1 part Kirschwasser

Splash of sloe gin

Shake with ice and strain into a cocktail glass.

SHERRY TWIST

2 parts cream sherry

1 part brandy

Dash of dry vermouth

Dash of triple sec

Shake with ice and strain into a cocktail glass.

SHERRY WHIZZ

1 part cream sherry
1 part orange juice
Splash of triple sec
1 egg white
Garnish: whipped cream
Shake with ice and strain into a cocktail glass. Garnish
with whipped cream.

SHINER

2 parts dark rum
1 part sambuca
Splash of lemon juice
Splash of grenadine
Shake with ice and strain into a cocktail glass.

SHINING STAR

1 part Passoã®
1 part grapefruit juice
Splash of gin
Splash of sweet vermouth
Stir with ice and strain into a cocktail glass.

SHINY NAIL

2 parts red wine
1 part Cointreau®
Pour into a wine glass and stir.

SHIRLEY TEMPLE

4 parts soda
1 part grenadine
Garnish: 2 cherries
Build on ice in a highball glass.
Garnish with 2 cherries.

SHITFACER

2 parts Bacardi Limon®
1 part Southern Comfort®
1 part vodka
Dash of dry vermouth
Garnish: lemon slice

Shake with ice and strain into a cocktail glass. Garnish with lemon slice.

SHIVA'S TEARS

1 part light rum
1 part Pisang Ambon®
1 part mango juice
Garnish: cherry

Shake with ice and strain into a cocktail glass. Garnish with cherry.

SHIVER

1 part vodka

1 part crème de banana

1 part Parfait Amour

Shake with ice and strain into a cocktail glass.

SHOE IN

1 part brandy

1 part grapefruit juice

1 part pineapple juice

Splash of light rum

Splash of dark rum

Splash of Bols® Maraschino

Shake with ice and strain into a cocktail glass.

SHOOT

1 part sherry

1 part scotch

Splash of lemon juice

Splash of orange juice

Pinch of sugar

Shake with ice and strain into a cocktail glass.

SHORTCAKE

1 part Frangelico®

1 part strawberry liqueur

1 part cream

Splash of Amaretto

Splash of triple sec

Shake with ice and strain into a cocktail glass.

SHORTCAKE CRUMBLE

2 parts coconut liqueur

2 parts cream

1 part strawberry liqueur

Splash of pineapple juice

Shake with ice and strain into a cocktail glass.

SHOTGUN WEDDING

1 part gin

1 part Dubonnet blonde

Splash of cherry brandy

Splash of orange juice

Stir with ice and strain into a cocktail glass.

SHOUT

1 part gin

1 part sweet vermouth

Splash of Chartreuse

Stir with ice and strain into a cocktail glass.

SHOW TIME

2 parts chocolate vodka
1 part peppermint schnapps
1 part tonic water
Splash of pineapple juice
Shake with ice and strain into a cocktail glass.

SHOWBIZ

2 parts vodka
2 parts grapefruit juice
1 part crème de cassis
Shake with ice and strain into a cocktail glass.

SHRINER COCKTAIL

1 part sloe gin
1 part plum brandy
1 tablespoon of syrup
Dash of bitters
Garnish: lemon twist
Shake with ice and strain into a cocktail glass.

SHUT UP

1 part vodka
1 part rum
Dash of dry vermouth
Dash of sweet vermouth
Shake with ice and strain into a cocktail glass.

SIBERIAN EXPRESS

2 parts espresso
1 part sweet vermouth
1 part coffee liqueur
Pinch of sugar
Shake with ice and strain into a cocktail glass.

SICILIAN KISS

3 parts Southern Comfort®
1 part Amaretto
Build on ice in a rocks glass.

SIDECAR

1 part brandy
1 part sour mix
Splash of triple sec
Garnish: sugar rim, orange slice and cherry
Shake with ice and strain into a sugar-rimmed cocktail
glass. Garnish with orange slice and cherry.

SIDELIGHT

2 parts cream
1 part whiskey
1 part coffee liqueur
1 part white crème de menthe
Shake with ice and strain into an Irish coffee glass.

SILENT BROADSIDER

2 parts light rum
1 part anisette
1 part banana juice
1 part grenadine
Shake with ice and strain into a cocktail glass.

SILENT THIRD

2 parts scotch
1 part raspberry liqueur
1 part grapefruit juice
Shake with ice and strain into a cocktail glass.

SILK NIGHTIE

2 parts tequila
2 parts cream
1 part white crème de cacao
1 part grenadine
Garnish: ground cinnamon
Shake with ice and strain into a cocktail glass. Dust
ground cinnamon on top.

SILK STOCKINGS

3 parts tequila
1 part brown crème de cacao
1 part Chambord®
1 part cream
Shake with ice and strain into a cocktail glass.

SILVER BULLET

1 part gin

Splash of scotch

Dash of dry vermouth

Garnish: lemon twist

Stir with ice and strain into a cocktail glass. Garnish
with lemon twist.

SILVER COCKTAIL

1 part gin

1 part tonic water

1 tablespoon of syrup

Dash of dry vermouth

Dash of bitters

Garnish: lemon twist

Stir with ice and strain into a cocktail glass. Garnish
with lemon twist.

SILVER JUBILEE

2 parts gin
1 part coffee liqueur
1 part cream
Stir with ice and strain into a cocktail glass.

SILVER KING COCKTAIL

2 parts Vana Tallinn®
1 part cream
1 egg white
Shake with ice and strain into a cocktail glass.

SILVER SPLINTER

1 part light rum
1 part sambuca
1 part advocaat
Shake with ice and strain into a cocktail glass.

SILVER STAR

1 part bourbon
Splash of cherry brandy
Splash of grenadine
Dash of dry vermouth
Garnish: cherry
Shake with ice and strain into a cocktail glass. Garnish
with cherry.

SILVER STREAK

2 parts gin
1 part Licor 43®
1 part advocaat
Stir with ice and strain into a cocktail glass.

SILVERADO

2 parts orange juice
1 part pomegranate vodka
1 part Campari®
Shake with ice and strain into a cocktail glass.

SIN INDUSTRIES

1 part vodka
1 part Bols® Blue
1 part triple sec
1 part grapefruit juice
Shake with ice and strain into a cocktail glass.

SINFULLY GOOD

1 part Bailey's Irish Cream®
1 part peppermint schnapps
1 part cream
1 tablespoon of chocolate syrup
Shake with ice and strain into a cocktail glass.

SINGAPORE

1 part gin
1 part Bols® Gold Strike
1 part sour mix
Garnish: blueberries
Stir with ice and strain into a cocktail glass. Garnish
with blueberries.

SINGAPORE SLING

3 parts sour mix
2 parts gin
1 part grenadine
1 part soda
Splash of cherry brandy
Build on ice in a tall glass and stir.

SINGE MALT MARTINI

3 part gin
1 part single malt scotch
Garnish: olive
Stir with ice and strain into a cocktail glass. Garnish
with olive.

SINGER

1 part peppermint schnapps
1 part Cognac
Splash of cherry brandy
Shake with ice and strain into a cocktail glass.

SINKHOLE

1 part Bailey's Irish Cream® Mint Chocolate
1 part Kahlua®
1 part brown crème de cacao
1 part coffee
Garnish: whipped cream
Pour into an Irish coffee glass and stir. Garnish with
whipped cream.

SINTERKLAAS

1 part Bols® Genever
1 part crème de cassis
1 part grenadine
1 part cream
Shake with ice and strain into a cocktail glass.

SIUSSESSE

1 part anisette
1 part peppermint schnapps
1 part tonic water
1 egg white
Shake with ice and strain into a cocktail glass.

SIZE ME UP

3 parts whiskey
1 part peach schnapps
1 part tonic water
Splash of lime juice
Shake with ice and strain into a cocktail glass.

SIZZLING MANIAC

2 parts peppermint schnapps
1 part beer
1 part grappa
Garnish: mint sprig
Shake with ice and strain into a cocktail glass. Garnish
with mint sprig.

SKINDY

2 parts champagne
1 part sloe gin
Pour into a champagne flute.

SKINNY DIP

2 parts beer
1 part vodka
Garnish: scoop of sherbert ice cream
Pour into a highball glass and stir. Top with scoop of
sherbert ice cream.

SKINNY DIPPER

2 parts cranberry juice
1 part Midori®
Splash of lime juice
Shake with ice and strain into a cocktail glass.

SKY PILOT

1 part amaro
1 part cinnamon schnapps
Pour into a wine glass and stir.

SKY SCRAPER

2 parts lemonade
1 part vodka
1 part pomegranate schnapps
Splash of grenadine
Garnish: lime wedge
Shake with ice and strain into a cocktail glass. Garnish
with lime wedge.

SLEDGEHAMMER

1 part dark rum
1 part coconut brandy
Splash of pastis
Shake with ice and strain into a cocktail glass.

SLEEP WELL

1 part brown crème de cacao
1 part coffee liqueur
1 part raspberry schnapps
1 part cream
Shake with ice and strain into a cocktail glass.

SLEEPY HEAD COCKTAIL

2 parts ginger ale
1 part brandy
1 part peppermint liqueur
Garnish: mint sprig
Shake with ice and strain into a cocktail glass. Garnish
with mint sprig.

SLEIGH RIDE

1 part tequila
1 part Chartreuse
1 part grenadine
Shake with ice and strain into a cocktail glass.

SLICE O'HEAVEN

2 parts apple juice
1 part Bols® Kiwi
1 part melon liqueur
Shake with ice and strain into a cocktail glass.

SLIPPERY NIPPLE COCKTAIL

3 parts sambuca
3 parts cream
1 part Bailey's Irish Cream®
Shake with ice and strain into a cocktail glass.

SLIPPERY SLOPE

3 parts orange juice
2 parts lemonade
1 part tequila
1 part Southern Comfort®
1 part sloe gin
Build on ice in a tall glass and stir.

SLIPPY NIPPY

2 parts grape juice
1 part Cognac
1 part Bols® Red Orange
Shake with ice and strain into a cocktail glass.

SLOE COACH

2 parts orange juice
1 part vodka
1 part Southern Comfort®
1 part sloe gin
Shake with ice and strain into a cocktail glass.

SLOE COMFORT

1 part gin
1 part Southern Comfort®
1 part sloe gin
Garnish: mint sprig
Stir with ice and strain into a cocktail glass. Garnish
with mint sprig.

SLOE COMFORTABLE SCREW

2 parts orange juice
1 part sloe gin
1 part Southern Comfort®
Build on ice in a highball glass.

SLOE COMFORTABLE SCREW AGAINST THE WALL

2 parts orange juice
1 part sloe gin
1 part Southern Comfort®
Splash of Galliano®
Pour sloe gin, Southern Comfort®, and orange juice
into a highball glass and stir. Top with Galliano®.

SLOE CURRANT

2 parts cream
1 part coffee liqueur
1 part crème de cassis
1 part sloe gin
Build on ice in a highball glass and stir.

SLOE DOWN

3 parts tequila

1 part sloe gin

1 part pineapple juice

Dash of sweet vermouth

Shake with ice and strain into a cocktail glass.

SLOE GIN FIZZ

3 parts sour mix

2 parts sloe gin

1 part soda

Garnish: cherry

Build on ice in a tall glass and stir.

Garnish with cherry.

SLOE RUM-AID

2 parts light rum
1 part sloe gin
1 part lemonade
Garnish: basil leaves
Shake with ice and strain into a cocktail glass. Garnish
with basil leaves.

SLOE SCREW

2 parts orange juice
1 part sloe gin
Build on ice in a highball glass.

SLOE SMACK IN THE FACE

2 parts orange juice
2 parts lemon-lime soda
1 part Southern Comfort®
1 part sloe gin
Splash of triple sec
Build on ice in a tall glass and stir.

SLOE TEQUILA

2 parts lemonade
1 part cranberry juice
1 part tequila
1 part sloe gin
1 part Malibu Coconut Rum®
Garnish: cherry
Build on ice in a tall glass and stir. Garnish with cherry.

SLOPPY JOE

1 part apricot brandy
1 part port wine
Splash of triple sec
Splash of grenadine
Splash of pineapple juice
Shake with ice and strain into a cocktail glass.

SLOW MOTION

2 parts orange juice
2 parts light rum
1 part Passoã®
1 part pineapple juice
Splash of grenadine
Build on ice in a tall glass and stir.

SMASH-UP

1 part scotch
1 tablespoon of honey
Dash of bitters
Garnish: mint sprig
Muddle mint sprig with honey in a rocks glass. Add ice,
pour scotch and bitters, and stir.

SMILEY FACE

2 parts gin

2 parts fruit punch

1 part blue curaçao

1 part Cointreau®

1 part peach juice

Build on ice in a tall glass and stir.

SMILING IVY

1 part peach schnapps

1 part light rum

1 part pineapple juice

1 egg white

Shake with ice and strain into a cocktail glass.

SMOKESCREEN

1 part dark rum
1 part cherry schnapps
1 part coconut liqueur
Splash of grenadine
Garnish: cherry

Shake with ice and strain into a cocktail glass. Garnish with cherry.

SMOOTH AND SEXY

2 parts orange juice
1 part passion fruit liqueur
1 part Amaretto
1 part blackberry juice

Build on ice in a tall glass and stir.

SMOOTH BLACK RUSSIAN

1 part vodka
1 part Kahlua®
Splash of cola
Splash of Guinness® Stout
Shake with ice and strain into a rocks glass.

SMOOTH OPERATOR

2 parts Cognac
1 part vanilla vodka
Splash of caramel liqueur
Shake with ice and strain into a cocktail glass.

SMOOTH PINK LEMONADE

3 parts vodka
1 part cranberry juice
Splash of sour mix
Splash of lemon-lime soda
Shake with ice and strain into a cocktail glass.

SMURF IN MEXICO

2 parts tequila
1 part blue curaçao
1 part pineapple juice
1 part coconut milk
Garnish: pineapple wedge
Build on ice in a highball glass and stir.
Garnish with pineapple wedge.

SNAKEBITE

1 part Yukon Jack®
Splash of lime juice
Garnish: lime wedge
Build on ice in a rocks glass.
Garnish with lime wedge.

SNOW MELTER

2 parts sambuca
1 part light rum
1 part white crème de cacao
Splash of cream
Shake with ice and strain into a cocktail glass.

SNOW SHOE

3 parts bourbon
1 part peppermint schnapps
Garnish: lime wedge
Build on ice in a rocks glass.
Garnish with lime wedge.

SNOW SUIT

1 part Dubonnet blonde
1 part brandy
1 part anisette
Garnish: cherry
Shake with ice and strain into a cocktail glass. Garnish
with cherry.

SNOWBALL

2 parts gin
1 part anisette
1 part cinnamon schnapps
1 part cream
Stir with ice and strain into a cocktail glass.

SO FRUITY

2 parts banana vodka
1 part strawberry liqueur
Splash of pineapple juice
Shake with ice and strain into a cocktail glass.

SO GINGY

2 parts whiskey
1 part Southern Comfort®
1 part ginger ale
Garnish: cherry
Shake with ice and strain into a cocktail glass. Garnish
with cherry.

SO IN LOVE

1 part chocolate vodka
1 part Parfait Amour
1 part Southern Comfort®
Garnish: cherry

Shake with ice and strain into a cocktail glass. Garnish with cherry.

SOFT MANHATTAN

2 parts Southern Comfort®
1 part sweet vermouth
Splash of grenadine
Dash of bitters
Garnish: cherry

Shake with ice and strain into a cocktail glass. Garnish with cherry.

SOFT ORGASM

1 part crème de banana
1 part cherry brandy
1 part grenadine
1 part cream
Shake with ice and strain into a cocktail glass.

SOLE ROSSO

2 parts Campari®
1 part grapefruit juice
Splash of blue curaçao
Shake with ice and strain into a rocks glass.

SOMETHING SASSY

2 parts sparkling wine
1 part chocolate liqueur
1 part sloe gin
Garnish: sugar rim
Pour into a sugar-rimmed champagne flute.

SON OF AGENT ORANGE

4 parts orange juice
1 part vodka
1 part gin
1 part whiskey
1 part apple schnapps
1 part melon liqueur
1 part soda
Build on ice in a tall glass and stir.

SONGBIRD

2 parts gin
2 parts Galliano®
1 part crème de banana
1 part pineapple juice
Stir with ice and strain into a rocks glass.

SOUL KISS

2 parts Dubonnet blonde

1 part orange juice

Dash of sweet vermouth

Dash of dry vermouth

Shake with ice and strain into a cocktail glass.

SOUR APPLE

2 parts applejack

1 part triple sec

1 part lemon juice

Splash of cranberry juice

Shake with ice and strain into a cocktail glass.

SOUTH BEACH

2 parts Cabana Boy® Vanilla Spice Rum

2 parts cream

1 part Kahlua®

Shake with ice and strain into a cocktail glass.

SOUTH BEACH COSMOPOLITAN

3 parts Absolut® Citron
1 part Chambord®
Splash of cranberry juice
Garnish: lemon wedge
Shake with ice and strain into a cocktail glass. Garnish
with lemon wedge.

SOUTH CAMP SPECIAL

1 part dark rum
1 part gin
1 part crème de noyaux
Splash of cream
Stir with ice and strain into a cocktail glass.

SOUTH OF THE BORDER COCKTAIL

2 parts lemonade
2 parts tequila
1 part triple sec
1 part lemon–lime soda
Splash of lime juice
Shake with ice and strain into a cocktail glass.

SOUTH PACIFIC

3 parts pineapple juice
2 parts coconut brandy
1 part vodka
Splash of grenadine
Build on ice in a highball glass and stir.

SOUTH SEAS APERITIF

2 parts melon liqueur
1 part crème de banana
1 part coconut liqueur
Splash of lime juice (freshly squeezed)
Shake with ice and strain into a cocktail glass.

SOUTH STREET COFFEE

2 parts coffee
2 parts light rum
1 part Bailey's Irish Cream® Mint Chocolate
Pour into an Irish coffee glass and stir.

SOUTHERN ITALIAN PISS

2 parts orange juice
1 part Southern Comfort®
1 part Amaretto
Splash of whiskey
Shake with ice and strain into a cocktail glass.

SOUTHERN MANHATTAN

1 part Southern Comfort®
Dash of dry vermouth
Garnish: cherry
Shake with ice and strain into a cocktail glass. Garnish
with cherry.

SOUTHERN SEÑORITA

2 parts Southern Comfort®
2 parts ginger ale
1 part tequila
1 part cola
Splash of lime juice
Build on ice in a highball glass and stir.

SOUTHERN STRAW

1 part Southern Comfort®
1 part grenadine
Shake with ice and strain into a brandy snifter.

SOUTHERN SUNRISE

2 parts Southern Comfort®
1 part grenadine
1 part lemon juice
1 part orange juice
Dash of bitters
Shake with ice and strain into a cocktail glass.

SOVIET COCKTAIL

2 parts amontillado
1 part vodka
1 part tonic water
Garnish: lemon twist
Shake with ice and strain into a cocktail glass. Garnish
with lemon twist.

SOVIET SPEAK

3 parts white wine
1 part blueberry vodka
Splash of grenadine
Pour into a wine glass and stir.

SPA

1 part Bombay Sapphire®
Splash of blue curaçao
Splash of tonic water
Stir with ice and strain into a cocktail glass.

SPACE

2 parts gin
1 part crème de banana
1 part Frangelico®
Stir with ice and strain into a cocktail glass.

SPACE ORBITER

2 parts grapefruit juice
1 part peppermint schnapps
1 part Amaretto
1 tablespoon of syrup
Shake with ice and strain into a cocktail glass.

SPARK IN THE NIGHT

2 parts dark rum
1 part Kahlua®
Splash of coffee liqueur
Splash of chocolate liqueur
Shake with ice and strain into a cocktail glass.

SPARKLING ROSE

2 parts sparkling wine
1 part cherry vodka
1 part pink lemonade
Garnish: cherry
Pour into a wine glass and stir. Garnish with cherry.

SPEARMINT IVAN

1 part vodka
Dash of dry vermouth
Garnish: mint sprig
Muddle vodka and mint sprig in a rocks glass. Add dry
vermouth and stir.

SPECIAL-TEA

2 parts iced tea
1 part peach schnapps
1 part Midori®
Garnish: lemon wedge
Shake with ice and strain into a cocktail glass. Garnish with lemon wedge.

SPHINX

2 parts gin
1 part sloe gin
1 part tonic water
1 part sweet vermouth
Stir with ice and strain into a cocktail glass.

SPICE IT UP

3 parts pineapple juice
1 part light rum
1 part spiced rum
1 part triple sec
Shake with ice and strain into a cocktail glass.

SPICE TO LIFE

1 part spiced rum

1 part Malibu Coconut Rum®

1 part orange juice

1 part cranberry juice

Shake with ice and strain into a cocktail glass.

SPICED BOUNTY

2 parts spiced rum

1 part peppermint schnapps

Splash of grenadine

Shake with ice and strain into a cocktail glass.

SPICED SWIZZLE

2 parts spiced rum

2 parts Bailey's Irish Cream®

1 part Amaretto

Splash of cream

Shake with ice and strain into a cocktail glass.

SPICED VANILLA WAFER

1 part vanilla liqueur
1 part spiced rum
1 part cream
Shake with ice and strain into a cocktail glass.

SPIDERMAN

2 parts peach vodka
1 part lime juice
1 part tonic water
Dash of bitters
Shake with ice and strain into a cocktail glass.

SPIKED BEER

1 part beer
1 part Absolut® Peppar
Splash of hot sauce
Build in a highball glass and stir.

SPIKED CAFÉ

2 parts dark rum
1 part Kahlua®
1 part light cream
Garnish: ground nutmeg
Shake with ice and strain into a cocktail glass. Garnish
with ground nutmeg.

SPIKED TEA

3 parts iced tea
1 part light rum
1 part dark rum
Garnish: lemon wedge
Shake with ice and strain into a cocktail glass. Garnish
with lemon wedge.

SPIRIT IN THE NIGHT

1 part Punt e Mes®
1 part orange juice
Shake with ice and strain into a cocktail glass.

SPRING FEELING

2 parts gin

1 part Chartreuse

1 part orange juice

1 part lemonade

Stir with ice and strain into a cocktail glass.

SPRITZER

1 part white wine

1 part soda

Pour into a wine glass.

SPUNK

2 parts tonic water

1 part gin

1 part green crème de menthe

Stir with ice and strain into a cocktail glass.

SPUNKY MONKEY

3 parts cream
1 part brown crème de cacao
1 part Kahlua®
1 part Frangelico®
Shake with ice and strain into a cocktail glass.

SPUTNIK

2 parts cream
2 parts peach vodka
1 part peach schnapps
1 part orange juice
Shake with ice and strain into a cocktail glass.

SQUEALING PINK SQUIRREL

2 parts crème de noyaux
1 part vodka
1 part cream
Shake with ice and strain into a cocktail glass.

SQUEEGE

2 parts cola
1 part bourbon
1 part Pisang Ambon®
Garnish: cherry
Shake with ice and strain into a cocktail glass. Garnish
with cherry.

ST. PATRICK'S DAY

1 part whiskey
1 part green crème de menthe
1 part Chartreuse
Dash of bitters
Shake with ice and strain into a cocktail glass.

STAR COCKTAIL

2 parts vodka
1 part maraschino liqueur
Dash of bitters
Shake with ice and strain into a cocktail glass.

STAY SAFE

1 part vodka
1 part blue curaçao
1 part cinnamon schnapps
1 part cranberry juice
Garnish: cinnamon stick
Serve hot in an Irish coffee glass. Garnish with cinnamon stick.

STEAMY AFTERNOON

2 parts lemonade
1 part gin
1 part Grand Marnier®
Garnish: lemon wedge
Shake with ice and strain into a cocktail glass.
Garnish with lemon wedge.

STIFFY

3 parts brandy

3 parts orange juice

1 part coffee liqueur

1 egg white

Shake with ice and strain into a wine glass.

STIMULANT

2 parts vodka

1 part cold coffee

Splash of butterscotch schnapps

Shake with ice and strain into a cocktail glass.

STINGAREE

1 part scotch

1 part Mandarine Napoléon®

1 part tonic water

1 tablespoon of honey

Shake with ice and strain into a cocktail glass.

STINGER

3 parts brandy
1 part white crème de menthe
Build on ice in a rocks glass.

STOCKHOLM 75

2 parts champagne
1 part Absolut® Citron
1 part lemonade
1 tablespoon of syrup
Pour into a champagne flute and stir.

STOMACH REVIVER

4 parts brandy
1 part fernet
Shake with ice and strain into a rocks glass.

STONE COLD PUNCH

1 part Southern Comfort®

1 part blackberry brandy

1 part cranberry juice

Shake with ice and strain into a cocktail glass.

STONE SOUR

1 part whiskey

1 part sour mix

1 part orange juice

Garnish: orange slice and cherry

Shake with ice and strain into a rocks glass. Garnish
with orange slice and cherry.

STOPLIGHT

1 part orange juice

1 part Pisang Ambon®

1 part raspberry liqueur

Shake with ice and strain into a cocktail glass.

STORM BREWING

2 parts spiced rum

1 part peppermint schnapps

1 part lemonade

1 part soda

Shake with ice and strain into a cocktail glass.

STRAIGHT UP

1 part Malibu Coconut Rum®

1 part Bailey's Irish Cream®

1 part butterscotch schnapps

Garnish: pineapple wedge

Shake with ice and strain into a cocktail glass. Garnish
with pineapple wedge.

STRANGER IN THE NIGHT

2 parts gin

1 part Parfait Amour

1 part orange juice

Splash of triple sec

1 egg white

Stir with ice and strain into a cocktail glass.

STRANGER IN TOWN

3 parts light rum

1 part sweet vermouth

1 part apple brandy

1 part cherry brandy

Garnish: cherry

Shake with ice and strain into a cocktail glass. Garnish
with cherry.

STRAWBERRY BLOND MARTINI

3 parts strawberry vodka

1 part Lillet

Splash of soda

Shake with ice and strain into a cocktail glass.

STRAWBERRY BUBBLE BATH

2 parts sparkling wine

1 part strawberry liqueur

Splash of vodka

Shake with ice and strain into a rocks glass.

STRAWBERRY BUTTERMILK

2 parts butterscotch schnapps

2 parts strawberry milk

1 part Frangelico®

Garnish: strawberry

Build on ice in a highball glass and stir.

Garnish with strawberry.

STRAWBERRY CAIPIRINHA

1 part cachaça
1 part strawberry liqueur
Shake with ice and strain into a cocktail glass.

STRAWBERRY CAKE

1 part strawberry liqueur
1 part cream
1 part yogurt
Pour into a highball glass filled with ice and stir until
yogurt is well blended.

STRAWBERRY DAIQUIRI

2 parts strawberry daiquiri mix
1 part light rum
Splash of sour mix
Garnish: sugar rim and whipped cream
Mix with ice in a blender and pour into a sugar-
rimmed glass. Garnish with whipped cream.

STRAWBERRY GIRL

2 parts Bols® Strawberry

1 part vanilla vodka

1 part white crème de cacao

Shake with ice and strain into a cocktail glass.

STRAWBERRY KIR ROYALE

2 parts champagne

1 part crème de cassis

1 tablespoon of strawberry syrup

Pour into a champagne flute and stir.

STRAWBERRY MARGARITA

3 parts tequila
3 parts sour mix
1 part strawberry liqueur
1 part grenadine
Garnish: salt rim and strawberry
Rim margarita glass with lime, then dip rim in salt.
Shake tequila, sour mix, strawberry liqueur, and grenadine with ice and strain into the salt-rimmed glass.
Garnish with strawberry.

STRAWBERRY SHORTCAKE

1 part Amaretto
1 part strawberry liqueur
1 scoop of vanilla ice cream
Garnish: whipped cream
Mix in a blender and pour into a highball glass. Garnish with whipped cream.

STRAWBERRY SOUR

2 parts sour mix
1 part scotch
1 part strawberry liqueur
Shake with ice and strain into a cocktail glass.

STRAWBERRY SUNRISE

2 parts orange juice
2 parts strawberry liqueur
Splash of grenadine
Build on ice in a highball glass and stir.

STRAWCHERRY

2 parts grape juice
1 part vodka
1 part strawberry liqueur
Splash of lemon juice
Shake with ice and strain into a cocktail glass.

STREET SCENE

1 part gin
1 part cherry brandy
Splash of hot sauce
Dash of dry vermouth
Shake with ice and strain into a cocktail glass.

STRETCHER BEARER

3 parts guava juice
1 part dark rum
1 part Malibu Coconut Rum®
1 part triple sec
1 part crème de banana
Build on ice in a highball glass and stir.

STUPID CUPID

1 part Absolut® Citron
1 part sloe gin
1 part sour mix
Shake with ice and strain into a cocktail glass.

SUE RIDING HIGH

3 parts dark rum

3 parts hot cocoa

1 part brown crème de cacao

Pour into an Irish coffee glass and stir.

SUEDE VIXEN

2 parts cream

1 part white crème de cacao

1 part Frangelico®

Splash of peppermint schnapps

Shake with ice and strain into a cocktail glass.

SUGAR DADDY

2 parts gin

2 parts maraschino liqueur

1 part pineapple juice

Dash of bitters

Shake with ice and strain into a cocktail glass.

SUICIDE

4 parts sour mix
1 part bourbon
1 part whiskey
1 part Southern Comfort®
1 part triple sec
Build on ice in a highball glass and stir.

SUMATRA JUICE

2 parts orange juice
1 part gin
Splash of apricot brandy
Splash of coffee brandy
Stir with ice and strain into a cocktail glass.

SUMMER BREEZE

2 parts Absolut® Citron
1 part melon liqueur
Splash of dry vermouth
Shake with ice and strain into a cocktail glass.

SUMMER SHADE

1 part vodka

1 part melon liqueur

1 part strawberry liqueur

Splash of soda

Shake with ice and strain into a cocktail glass.

SUN AND FUN

2 parts tequila

1 part crème de banana

1 part lemonade

Splash of tonic water

Shake with ice and strain into a cocktail glass.

SUN DECK

1 part vodka

1 part Campari®

Dash of dry vermouth

Dash of bitters

Shake with ice and strain into a cocktail glass.

SUN OF A BEACH

2 parts orange juice
1 part gin
1 part Midori®
Stir with ice and strain into a cocktail glass.

SUNBURN

2 parts tequila
2 parts cranberry juice
1 part triple sec
Build on ice in a highball glass.

SUNDOWN

3 parts pineapple juice
1 part vodka
1 part apricot brandy
Build on ice in a highball glass and stir.

SUNNY BEACH

2 parts white wine
1 part blackberry schnapps
Pour into a wine glass.

SUNNY ISLAND

2 parts mango juice
1 part light rum
Shake with ice and strain into a cocktail glass.

SUNSET BEACH

2 parts pineapple juice
1 part melon liqueur
1 part Bols® Coconut
Shake with ice and strain into a cocktail glass.

SUNSPLASH

2 parts orange juice
1 part Malibu Coconut Rum®
1 part Chambord®
1 part peach schnapps
Build on ice in a highball glass and stir.

SUPER GENIUS

3 parts blueberry vodka
1 part grenadine
1 part soda
Shake with ice and strain into a cocktail glass.

SUPERCAIPI

2 parts cachaça
1 part vanilla liqueur
Shake with ice and strain into a cocktail glass.

SURFER ON ACID COCKTAIL

2 parts Malibu Coconut Rum®
1 part Jägermeister®
1 part pineapple juice
Shake with ice and strain into a cocktail glass.

SURFSIDE SWINGER

1 part light rum
1 part gin
1 part passion fruit juice
Shake with ice and strain into a cocktail glass.

SURPRISE

2 parts gin
1 part Drambuie®
1 part orange juice
Dash of bitters
Stir with ice and strain into a cocktail glass.

SUZE TROPIC

3 parts soda
2 parts white wine
Splash of lime juice (freshly squeezed)
Pour into a wine glass and stir.

SWAMP WATER

1 part vodka
1 part Bols® Blue
1 part Galliano®
Shake with ice and strain into a cocktail glass.

SWEAT HEAT

2 parts orange juice
1 part crème de cassis
1 part Pisang Ambon®
1 part Bols® Coconut
Build on ice in a highball glass and stir.

SWEDISH FISH

1 part blackberry schnapps
Splash of cranberry juice
Splash of sour mix
Shake with ice and strain into a rocks glass.

SWEDISH LADY

1 part vodka
1 part Bols® Strawberry
1 tablespoon of sugar
Splash of cream
Shake with ice and strain into a cocktail glass.

SWEET AND BLUE

3 parts sour mix
1 part raspberry liqueur
1 part melon liqueur
Build on ice in a highball glass and stir.

SWEET CHARGE

2 parts Southern Comfort®
2 parts strawberry-kiwi juice
Build on ice in a highball glass and stir.

SWEET CONCOCTION

3 parts soda
2 parts Amaretto
2 parts peach schnapps
Splash of sweet vermouth
Build on ice in a highball glass and stir.

SWEET DREAM COCKTAIL

3 parts vodka
2 parts coconut milk
1 part orange juice
1 egg white
Shake with ice and strain into a cocktail glass.

SWEET DUMBO

1 part light rum
1 part triple sec
1 part peppermint schnapps
1 part cream
Shake with ice and strain into a cocktail glass.

SWEET EDEN

2 parts Cognac
1 part coffee liqueur
1 part orange juice
Garish: cherry
Shake with ice and strain into a cocktail glass. Garnish
with cherry.

SWEET FLAMINGO

2 parts gin
2 parts pineapple juice
2 parts orange juice
1 part coconut milk
Build on ice in a highball glass and stir.

SWEET HARMONY

2 parts vodka
2 parts melon liqueur
1 part kiwi liqueur
Garnish: kiwi slice
Shake with ice and strain into a cocktail glass. Garnish
with kiwi slice.

SWEET SMELL OF SUCCESS

3 parts lemonade
1 part Passoã®
1 part Campari®
Shake with ice and strain into a cocktail glass.

SWEET TALKER

2 parts raspberry liqueur
2 parts cream
1 part Southern Comfort®
Shake with ice and strain into a cocktail glass.

SWEET TART

3 parts sour mix
1 part blackberry brandy
1 part Southern Comfort®
Garnish: orange slice and cherry
Build on ice in a tall glass and stir. Garnish with orange
slice and cherry.

SWEET TEMPTATION

2 parts banana vodka
1 part soda
1 part orange juice
Splash of grenadine
Garnish: orange slice
Shake with ice and strain into a cocktail glass. Garnish
with orange slice.

SWEET, SOUR, AND SPICE

2 parts lemonade
1 part melon liqueur
1 part ginger liqueur
Shake with ice and strain into a cocktail glass.

SWEETEST PERFECTION

1 part vodka
1 light rum
1 part fruit punch
Shake with ice and strain into a cocktail glass.

SWEETHEART

1 part Parfait Amour
1 part Amaretto
1 part vanilla liqueur
1 part cream
Shake with ice and strain into a cocktail glass.

SWEETIE PIE

2 parts kiwi liqueur

1 part gin

1 part orange juice

Stir with ice and strain into a cocktail glass.

SWEETS FOR MY SWEET

2 parts Disaronno®

1 part white crème de cacao

1 part strawberry liqueur

Shake with ice and strain into a cocktail glass.

TABOO

2 parts Disaronno®
1 part cream
Shake with ice and strain into a rocks glass.

TAME BULLDOG

1 part whiskey
1 part chocolate liqueur
1 part Amaretto
1 part cola
Shake with ice and strain into a cocktail glass.

TART PUNCH

1 part Jack Daniel's®
1 part Southern Comfort®
1 part Chambord®
1 part sour mix
1 part lemon-lime soda
Shake with ice and strain into a cocktail glass.

TASTY TREAT

2 parts cola
1 part vanilla vodka
Splash of Tuaca®
Build on ice in a highball glass and stir.

TATTOOED LOVE GODDESS

2 parts chocolate liqueur
1 part raspberry vodka
1 part vanilla liqueur
1 part coconut milk
Shake with ice and strain into a cocktail glass.

TAWNY

2 parts chocolate vodka

1 part blackberry schnapps

Splash of cream

Garnish: chocolate rim

Shake with ice and strain into a chocolate-rimmed
cocktail glass.

TEAM PLAYER

2 parts vodka

1 part peach schnapps

1 part Irish cream

Splash of sour mix

Shake with ice and strain into a cocktail glass.

TEAM WORK

2 parts iced tea

1 part vodka

1 part triple sec

Garnish: lemon wedge

Shake with ice and strain into a rocks glass. Garnish
with lemon wedge.

TEDDY BEAR

1 part vodka

1 part cinnamon schnapps

1 part Bols® Lychee

Shake with ice and strain into a cocktail glass.

TEN GALLON COCKTAIL

1 part gin

1 part coffee liqueur

Splash of sweet vermouth

1 egg white

Stir with ice and strain into a cocktail glass.

TENDERNESS

1 part whiskey
1 part peach schnapps
1 part Amaretto
Splash of lime juice
Shake with ice and strain into a cocktail glass.

TEQUILA MOCKINGBIRD

3 parts tequila
1 part triple sec
1 part blue curaçao
Splash of cranberry juice
Splash of orange juice
Garnish: salt rim and lime wedge
Rim margarita glass with lime, then dip rim
in salt. Shake tequila, triple sec, blue curaçao, cranberry
juice, and orange juice with ice
and strain into the salt-rimmed glass.
Garnish with lime wedge.

TEQUILA SUNRISE

2 parts orange juice

1 part tequila

Splash of grenadine

Pour orange juice and tequila into a highball glass and stir. Float grenadine around edge of glass.

THAT'S A WRAP

2 parts banana vodka

1 part orange juice

Garnish: orange slice

Shake with ice and strain into a cocktail glass. Garnish with orange slice.

THAT'S LIFE

2 parts light rum

Splash of passion fruit juice

Splash of pear juice

1 egg white

Shake with ice and strain into a cocktail glass.

THAT'S PRETTY

2 parts grape soda
1 part Absolut® Kurant
Build on ice in a highball glass and stir.

THIS WILL MESS YOU UP

1 part grappa
1 part tonic water
Shake with ice and strain into a cocktail glass.

THREE COUNTS

1 part vodka
1 part hazelnut liqueur
1 part crème de banana
Splash of Campari®
Shake with ice and strain into a cocktail glass.

THREE MORE PLEASE

2 parts blueberry vodka

1 part soda

1 part sloe gin

Splash of lemon juice

Garnish: lemon twist

Shake with ice and strain into a cocktail glass. Garnish with lemon twist.

THUNDER

1 part brandy

1 egg white

Pinch of sugar

Pinch of cayenne pepper

Shake with ice and strain into a cocktail glass.

TIGER BALM

3 parts Bols® Genever
1 part vanilla liqueur
Garnish: lemon twist
Shake with ice and strain into a cocktail glass. Garnish
with lemon twist.

TIME TO SPARE

2 parts whiskey
1 part port wine
1 part grenadine
1 egg white
Shake with ice and strain into a cocktail glass.

TIPPERARY

1 part whiskey
1 part ginger liqueur
1 part sweet vermouth
Shake with ice and strain into a cocktail glass.

T-N-T

2 parts tonic water

1 part Tanqueray®

Garnish: lime wedge

Build on ice in a highball glass. Garnish with lime wedge.

TOASTED ALMOND

3 parts Amaretto

1 part Kahlua®

Splash of cream

Build on ice in a rocks glass.

TOBACCO ROAD

2 parts Southern Comfort®

1 part orange juice

1 part beer

Shake with ice and strain into a cocktail glass.

TOM COLLINS

3 parts sour mix
2 parts gin
1 part soda
Garnish: orange slice and cherry
Build on ice in a tall glass and stir. Garnish with orange slice and cherry.

TOOTSIE ROLL MARTINI

3 parts sweet vermouth
1 part brown crème de cacao
Shake with ice and strain into a cocktail glass.

TORNADO

1 part bourbon
Splash of fernet
Shake with ice and strain into a cocktail glass.

TOUCHDOWN

1 part vodka

1 part apricot brandy

1 part pink lemonade

Shake with ice and strain into a cocktail glass.

TOVARICH

2 parts vodka

1 part Kümmel

Splash of lime juice

Shake with ice and strain into a cocktail glass.

TOWN AND COUNTRY

1 part whiskey

1 part crème de cassis

1 part orange juice

Splash of sour mix

Shake with ice and strain into a cocktail glass.

TRANSYLVANIAN MARTINI

2 parts vodka
1 part blackberry schnapps
Splash of pineapple juice
Shake with ice and strain into a cocktail glass.

TREASURY

2 parts tomato juice
1 part tequila
1 part cola
Build on ice in a highball glass and stir.

TREATS ALL AROUND

2 parts butterscotch schnapps
2 parts cream
1 part caramel liqueur
1 part white crème de cacao
Garnish: cherry
Build on ice in a highball glass and stir.
Garnish with cherry.

TREMBLER

2 parts mango juice

1 part light rum

1 part Amaretto

Shake with ice and strain into a cocktail glass.

TRIFECTA

1 part light rum

1 part Dubonnet blonde

Splash of lemon juice

Shake with ice and strain into a cocktail glass.

TRIPLE COFFEE

2 parts triple sec

1 part Bailey's Irish Cream®

1 part coffee

Garnish: whipped cream

Pour into an Irish coffee glass.

Garnish with whipped cream.

TRIPLE XYZ

2 parts Captain Morgan's® Parrot Bay
1 part raspberry liqueur
1 part pineapple juice
Shake with ice and strain into a cocktail glass.

TROPICAL CACHAÇA

1 part cachaça
1 part coffee liqueur
1 part Amaretto
Splash of pineapple juice
Shake with ice and strain into a cocktail glass.

TROPICAL CREAM

2 parts light rum
1 part Bols® Coconut
1 part mango juice
Shake with ice and strain into a cocktail glass.

TROPICAL HIT

2 parts orange juice
1 part triple sec
1 part mango schnapps
Build on ice in a highball glass and stir.

TROPICAL ITCH

2 parts tequila
1 part triple sec
1 part mango juice
Garnish: lemon slice
Shake with ice and strain into a cocktail glass. Garnish
with lemon slice.

TROPICAL LIFESAVER COCKTAIL

2 parts Absolut® Citron
1 part Malibu Coconut Rum®
1 part melon liqueur
Splash of sour mix
Splash of pineapple juice
Shake with ice and strain into a cocktail glass.

TROPICAL MELODY

1 part Bacardi® Limón
1 part light rum
1 part strawberry kiwi juice
Shake with ice and strain into a cocktail glass.

TROPICAL PEACH SODA

1 part Malibu Coconut Rum®
1 part peach schnapps
1 part ginger ale
Shake with ice and strain into a cocktail glass.

TROPICAL WAVE

1 part mango vodka
1 part Passoã®
1 part mango juice
Shake with ice and strain into a cocktail glass.

TROPICS

3 parts iced tea
1 part mango vodka
1 part crème de banana
Build on ice in a highball glass and stir.

TRUE BEAUTY

2 parts cream
1 part Frangelico®
1 part Pama®
Shake with ice and strain into a cocktail glass.

TRULY DELIGHTFUL

2 parts white grape juice
1 part vodka
1 part sloe gin
1 part peach schnapps
Build on ice in a highball glass and stir.

TRUTH SERUM

2 parts vodka

1 part coffee liqueur

1 part sherry

Splash of lime juice

Shake with ice and strain into a cocktail glass.

TUMMY BLOWER

3 parts Bailey's Irish Cream®

1 part root beer

Build on ice in a highball glass and stir.

TURBO CHANDY

2 parts sparkling wine

1 part Red Bull®

Pour into a wine glass and stir.

TURN A NEW LEAF

1 part Cointreau®
1 part pineapple juice
Splash of tonic water
Garnish: basil leaves
Build on ice in a highball glass and stir. Garnish with
basil leaves.

TURNCOAT

1 part light rum
1 part vodka
1 part Parfait Amour
Splash of lime juice
Shake with ice and strain into a cocktail glass.

TUTU DIVINE

2 parts grapefruit juice
1 part peach schnapps
Splash of Campari®
Pinch of sugar
Shake with ice and strain into a cocktail glass.

TUXEDO JUNCTION

1 part gin
1 part dry vermouth
1 part maraschino liqueur
Splash of pastis
Dash of bitters
Stir with ice and strain into a cocktail glass.

TWISTED

2 parts Cognac
1 part triple sec
1 part maraschino liqueur
Shake with ice and strain into a cocktail glass.

TWO LOVERS

2 parts light rum
Splash of Parfait Amour
Shake with ice and strain into a cocktail glass.

ULTIMATE CHALLENGE

2 parts Bols® Lychee
1 part Bols® Chocolate Mint
1 part Bols® Coconut
1 tablespoon of caramel syrup
Splash of Amaretto
Shake with ice and strain into a cocktail glass.

UNBELIEVABLE

2 parts gin
1 part apple schnapps
1 part orange juice
Garnish: orange slice
Stir with ice and strain into a cocktail glass. Garnish
with orange slice.

UNDERTAKER

1 part whiskey
1 part grenadine
Splash of butterscotch schnapps
Shake with ice and strain into a cocktail glass.

UNLIMITED

3 parts brandy
Splash of apple schnapps
Splash of soda
Shake with ice and strain into a cocktail glass.

UPSTREAM

1 part sparkling wine
1 part light rum
1 part raspberry liqueur
Pinch of sugar
Pour into a wine glass and stir.

VACATION

2 parts cranberry juice
1 part whiskey
1 part Southern Comfort®
Build on ice in a tall glass and stir.

VACATION TIME

2 parts tequila
2 parts Grand Marnier®
1 part peach schnapps
1 part cranberry juice
Shake with ice and strain into a cocktail glass.

VALENCIA MARTINI

3 parts gin
1 part sherry
Splash of crème de cassis
Stir with ice and strain into a cocktail glass.

VAMPIRE

1 part vodka
1 part Chambord®
1 part lime juice
1 part cranberry juice
Shake with ice and strain into a cocktail glass.

VANILICIOUS

3 parts light rum
1 part Licor 43®
Garnish: ground cinnamon
Shake with ice and strain into a cocktail glass. Garnish
with ground cinnamon.

VANILLA BERRY LEMONADE

2 parts lemonade
1 part spiced rum
1 part crème de cassis
1 part Bols® Vanilla
1 tablespoon of syrup
Shake with ice and strain into a cocktail glass.

VANILLA CREAMSICLE

1 part vanilla liqueur
Splash of triple sec
Splash of orange juice
Shake with ice and strain into a cocktail glass.

VANILLA NUT

1 part Licor 43®
Splash of Amaretto
Shake with ice and strain into a cocktail glass.

VANILLA RUNNER

2 parts dark rum
1 part Licor 43®
1 part pineapple juice
Shake with ice and strain into a cocktail glass.

VELVET HAMMER

2 parts cream
1 part white crème de cacao
1 part triple sec
Shake with ice and strain into a cocktail glass.

VENETIAN MOONLIGHT

2 parts vodka
2 parts Parfait Amour
1 part Aperol
1 tablespoon of strawberry syrup
Dash of dry vermouth
Garnish: strawberry
Shake with ice and strain into a cocktail glass. Garnish
with strawberry.

VERY COMFORTABLE

2 parts apple juice
1 part Southern Comfort®
1 part Amaretto
Shake with ice and strain into a cocktail glass.

VERY FRUITY

1 part vodka
1 part peach schnapps
1 part sloe gin
1 part lemonade
1 part lemon-lime soda
Shake with ice and strain into a cocktail glass.

VIKING FANTASY

1 part Bailey's Irish Cream® Mint Chocolate
1 part coffee liqueur
1 part cream
Garnish: chocolate syrup rim
Shake with ice and strain into a chocolate-rimmed
cocktail glass.

VODKA INFUSION

1 part vodka
1 part scotch
1 part Bailey's Irish Cream®
1 part brown crème de cacao
Shake with ice and strain into a cocktail glass.

VODKA SAKETINI

1 part vodka
Splash of sake
Garnish: lemon twist
Shake with ice and strain into a cocktail glass. Garnish
with lemon twist.

VOILÀ

4 parts vodka
1 part peach schnapps
Splash of lemon-lime soda
Garnish: lemon twist
Shake with ice and strain into a cocktail glass. Garnish
with lemon twist.

WACKED-OUT FRUIT

2 parts Pisang Ambon®
1 part lemon schnapps
1 part grapefruit juice

Shake with ice and strain into a cocktail glass.

WAIKIKI

2 parts orange juice
1 part light rum
1 part Passoã®
Splash of Campari®

Shake with ice and strain into a cocktail glass.

WAKE UP COCKTAIL

2 parts cream
1 part watermelon liqueur
1 part white crème de cacao
Shake with ice and strain into a cocktail glass.

WARM WELCOME

1 part Bols® Red Orange
1 part guava juice
Splash of vodka
Garnish: cherry
Shake with ice and strain into a cocktail glass. Garnish
with cherry.

WARSAW

3 parts vodka
1 part pomegranate schnapps
1 part soda
Dash of dry vermouth
Shake with ice and strain into a cocktail glass.

WASHINGTON APPLE COCKTAIL

1 part Crown Royal®

1 part apple schnapps

1 part cranberry juice

1 part lemonade

Shake with ice and strain into a cocktail glass.

WATERMELON MARTINI

2 parts watermelon vodka

1 part cherry brandy

1 part sweet vermouth

Shake with ice and strain into a cocktail glass.

WATERMELON SODA

2 parts lemon-lime soda

1 part watermelon vodka

Splash of lime juice

Shake with ice and strain into a cocktail glass.

WATERMELON SPRITZER

2 parts white wine
1 part watermelon vodka
1 part Midori®
Splash of soda
Pour into a wine glass and stir.

WEDDING BELLE

2 parts cherry brandy
1 part gin
1 part Dubonnet blonde
Pinch of sugar
Shake with ice and strain into a cocktail glass.

WEIRDED OUT

1 part Malibu Coconut Rum®
1 part kiwi liqueur
1 part pineapple juice
Shake with ice and strain into a cocktail glass.

WET DREAM

2 parts cherry brandy
1 part gin
1 part sweet vermouth
Garnish: cherry
Shake with ice and strain into a cocktail glass. Garnish
with cherry.

WHAT TRANSPIRES

2 parts gin
1 part sherry
1 part orange juice
Stir with ice and strain into a cocktail glass.

WHATEVER

1 part tequila
1 part strawberry liqueur
Splash of Campari®
Splash of grenadine
Shake with ice and strain into a cocktail glass.

WHISKEY SOUR

2 parts sour mix
1 part whiskey
Garnish: orange slice and cherry
Shake with ice and strain into a rocks glass. Garnish
with orange slice and cherry.

WHITE RUSSIAN

3 parts vodka
1 part Kahlua®
Splash of cream
Build on ice in a rocks glass.

WHITE SANGRIA COCKTAIL

2 parts sparkling wine
1 part light rum
1 part mango juice
Splash of Grand Marnier®
Garnish: cinnamon stick
Pour into a wine glass and stir. Garnish with cinnamon
stick.

WICKED TASTY TREAT

1 part cinnamon vodka

1 part Amaretto

1 part Kahlua®

1 part Bailey's Irish Cream® Mint Chocolate

1 part cream

Garnish: cinnamon stick

Shake with ice and strain into a cocktail glass. Garnish with cinnamon stick.

WIDOW'S DREAM COCKTAIL

2 parts Bénédictine

1 part cream

1 egg

Mix Bénédictine and egg well. Pour into a wine glass and add cream.

WEIRD WILLY

2 parts orange soda
1 part Absolut® Citron
1 part light rum
Build on ice in a highball glass and stir.

WILD WILD WEST

2 parts Malibu Coconut Rum®
1 part mango schnapps
1 part pear juice
Splash of vodka
Shake with ice and strain into a cocktail glass.

WINDY CITY

2 parts vodka
1 part Parfait Amour
1 part blue curaçao
Shake with ice and strain into a cocktail glass.

WINE COOLER

1 part red wine
1 part soda
Pour into a wine glass.

WINE REFRESHMENT

1 part white wine
1 part pineapple juice
Splash of grenadine
Garnish: pineapple wedge
Shake with ice and strain into a wine glass. Garnish
with pineapple wedge.

WINE TRUFFLE

2 parts crème de noyaux
1 part white wine
1 part Cognac
Pour into a wine glass.

WINNING STREAK

2 parts white wine

1 part crème de banana

Splash of triple sec

Garnish: cinnamon sticks

Pour into a wine glass and stir. Garnish with cinnamon sticks.

WISE CHOICE

1 part whiskey

1 part Chartreuse

1 part sweet vermouth

Shake with ice and strain into a cocktail glass.

WITCH'S WINE

2 parts Strega®

1 part sparkling wine

1 part white crème de cacao

Build on ice in a highball glass and stir.

WITH SUSHI

1 part gin
1 part sake
1 part triple sec
Shake with ice and strain into a cocktail glass.

WOMANIZER

1 part gin
Splash of Parfait Amour
Splash of cherry brandy
Splash of lime juice
Garnish: lemon twist
Stir with ice and strain into a cocktail glass. Garnish
with lemon twist.

WOO WOO COCKTAIL

3 parts vodka
1 part peach schnapps
1 part cranberry juice
Garnish: cranberries
Build on ice in a highball glass and stir. Garnish with
cranberries.

WOW

1 part Jack Daniel's®
1 part Rumple Minze®
Shake with ice and strain into a cocktail glass.

XANADU

1 part gin
1 part cherry brandy
1 part Chartreuse
Stir with ice and strain into a sugar-rimmed
cocktail glass.

YES WE HAVE NO BANANAS

1 part light rum
1 part crème de banana
Splash of lime juice
Splash of triple sec
Garnish: cherry
Shake with ice and strain into a cocktail glass.

YESTERDAY

2 parts pineapple juice
2 parts bourbon
1 part crème de banana
Splash of grenadine
Shake with ice and strain into a cocktail glass.

YOU'RE A DOLL

2 parts banana juice

1 part light rum

1 part blackberry schnapps

Splash of peach schnapps

Build on ice in a highball glass and stir.

YOUR ADVOCATE

2 parts crème de banana

1 part melon liqueur

1 part advocaat

Garnish: cherry

Shake with ice and strain into a cocktail glass. Garnish
with cherry.

YOWLING TOMCAT

3 parts tequila
1 part Bols® Lychee
1 part orange juice
Shake with ice and strain into a cocktail glass.

YUM

2 parts coconut rum
2 parts Pama®
1 part pineapple juice
Shake with ice and strain into a cocktail glass.

ZIGGURAT

3 parts red wine
1 part triple sec
1 part cream sherry
Pour into a wine glass and stir.

ZOMBIE

2 parts sour mix

2 parts orange juice

1 part light rum

1 part dark rum

1 part triple sec

1 part crème de noyaux

Splash of soda

Splash of Bacardi 151®

Garnish: orange slice and cherry

Build on ice in a tall glass and stir.

Top with Bacardi 151®. Garnish with orange slice and cherry.

ZOMBIE RETURNS

1 part pineapple juice
1 part orange juice
1 part sour mix
1 part light rum
1 part dark rum
1 part amber rum
Splash of soda
Splash of Bacardi 151®
Garnish: pineapple wedge
Build on ice in a tall glass and stir. Top with Bacardi 151®. Garnish with pineapple wedge.

ZORBATINI

1 part vodka
Splash of ouzo
Shake with ice and strain into a cocktail glass.

INDEX

208; Jelly Bean, 224; Ladies Cocktail, 239; Merry Widow Cocktail, 269; Morning Cocktail, 297; Mother of Pearl, 299; New Orleans Cocktail, 314; Oyster Bay, 340; Pansy Blossom Cocktail, 346; Rattlesnake Cocktail, 402; Repair Kit, 414; Rock Thrower, 420; Rolls Royce, 422; Schvitzer, 455; Scottish Runner, 460; Shanghai Cocktail, 476; Silent Broadsider, 488; Siussesse, 496; Snow Suit, 511; Snowball, 512

APEROL, in Bamboleo Papa Shake, 64; Bananafana, 68; Dean Martini, 137; Grand Soda, 188; Keep Quiet, 232; Mr. Dry, 302; Mutziputzi, 306; Venetian Moonlight, 584

APFELKORN, in Apple Orchard, 54; Caribbean Fruit Orgy, 110; Sex in Greece, 471

APPLE BRANDY, in Angel Face, 52; Apple Blow Fizz, 53; Apple Orchard, 54; Betrayed, 73; Brandywine, 92; Deauville, 137; Empire, 153; Especially Rough, 154; Granddaddy, 188; Honeymoon Cocktail, 206; Horny Bastard, 208; Jersey Lightning, 225; Madame Butterfly, 256; Old Car, 330; Paradise Bay, 347; Polynesian Apple, 375; Saucy Sue, 451; Savoy Tango, 452; Scotch Lemonade, 458; Stranger in Town, 536

ARMAGNAC, in Love Italian Style, 252; Mon Ami, 289; Paris Love, 348; Satin Doll, 451

BAILEY'S IRISH CREAM®, in Alaskan Monk, 46; B-53, 60; BMW, 88; Brain Cocktail, 91; Bring It On, 95; Butterworth, 96; Buttery Nipple Cocktail, 96; Catch Me If You Can, 111; Coffee Fraise, 124; Drag, 145; Fluff Cocktail, 160; Galaxy, 169; Ghostbuster, 175; Irish Colonel, 217; Irish Cream Freeze, 217; Irish Gingy, 217; Keep It Clean, 231; Lemon Cake, 242; Mellow Out, 266; Midnight Wakeup, 273; Milk and Honey, 275; Milky Way Martini, 275; Mint Cream Pie, 277; Monk's Martini, 290; More Fun Than a Barrel of Monkeys, 296; Muddy Waters, 304; Mudslide, 304; Nutty Irishman, 327; Oatmeal Cookie, 329; Panty Dropper, 346; Peachy Cream, 354; Roman Snowball, 423; Root of Things, 425; Rushing, 435; Screaming Cream Special, 461; Sinfully Good, 493; Slippery Nipple Cocktail, 500; Spiced Swizzle, 525; Straight Up, 535; Triple Coffee, 571; Tummy Blower, 576; Vodka Infusion, 586

BAILEY'S IRISH CREAM® **MINT CHOCOLATE**, Russian Haze, 437; Sinkhole, 495; South Street Coffee, 519; Viking Fantasy, 585; Wicked Tasty Treat, 593

BANANA LIQUEUR, in Banana Dream, 66; Gimme More, 176; Iceberg in Radioactive Water, 212; Jamaican Me Crazy, 223; Jolly

Baron, 419; Rolls Royce, 422; Ruby Red, 429; Rye and Dry, 439; Sambuca Blitz, 445; San Francisco Cocktail, 446; Scotch Bishop, 457; Screaming Viking, 462; Señor Jacques, 467; Sexy Devil, 474; Shamrock, 475; Sharona, 478; Sherry Twist, 479; Shitfacer, 482; Shut Up, 487; Silver Bullet, 490; Silver Cocktail, 490; Silver Star, 492; Soul Kiss, 516; Southern Manhattan, 519; Spearmint Ivan, 523; Street Scene, 542; Summer Breeze, 544; Sun Deck, 545; Tuxedo Junction, 578; Venetian Moonlight, 584; Warsaw, 588

VERMOUTH, SWEET, in Adonis Cocktail, 43; Affinity Cocktail, 44; Afternoon Pleasure, 45; Baja California Dream, 62; Colonel's Choice, 126; Crazy Frenchman, 131; Daily Double C, 134; Damn the Weather Martini, 135; Devil Cocktail, 141; Dream in Scarlet, 146; Exotic Tulip, 156; Frog in a Strawberry Field, 163; Geez Louise, 171; Hankhattan, 197; Hat Trick, 199; Hoot Mon, 207; Intrigue Cocktail, 216; Irish Cheer, 216; Irish Gingy, 217; Italian Stallion, 220; Jersey Lightning, 225; Jet Black, 225; Keep Quiet, 232; Leap Year, 241; Lord Byron, 250; Luxury, 254; Manhattan, 263; Merry Widow Cocktail, 269; Million Dollar Cocktail, 276; Mint Punch, 280; Mombasa, 289; Montmartre, 292; Moulin Rouge, 300; Mountain Cocktail, 301; Mozart, 302; Mr. New York, 303; Negroni, 310; Never Again, 313; Norwegian Summer, 324;

Raspberry Kamikaze, 400; Raspberry Passion, 401; Razzmopolitan, 403; Ready or Not, 403; Reality Bites, 404; Red Apple, 406; Red Devil, 407; Red Dog Martini, 408; Red Panties, 409; Red Russian, 410; Relax, 413; Rip the Sheets Orgasm, 417; Robber Baron, 419; Rose-Colored Glass, 426; Royal Palace, 428; Rushin' Around, 435; Russian Apple, 436; Russian Bear Cocktail, 436; Russian Gold, 436; Russian Haze, 437; Russian Jack, 437; Russian Nut, 437; Russian Suntan, 438; Russian Turbulence, 438; Saga Special, 440; Salem Witch, 442; Salty Dog, 443; Samba, 444; Sambucatini, 445; Santa Claus, 448; Satin Angel, 450; Save Me, 452; Save the Planet, 452; Scarlet Crusher, 454; Screaming Cream Special, 461; Screaming Georgia Butter, 461; Screw Me, 462; Screwdriver, 462; Sea Breeze, 463; See Ya Later, 465; Seether, 466; Serenade, 467; Sex on the Beach, 472; Sex on the Kitchen Floor, 472; Sex Under the Sun, 473; Sexy Devil, 474; Shag in the Sand, 474; Shake Hands, 474; Shark Attack, 476; Shark's Breath, 477; Sheer Elegance, 478; Shitfacer, 482; Shiver, 483; Showbiz, 486; Shut Up, 487; Sin Industries, 493; Skinny Dip, 497; Sky Scraper, 498; Sloe Coach, 501; Smooth Black Russian, 509; Smooth Pink Lemonade, 509; Son of Agent Orange, 515; South Pacific, 518; Soviet Cocktail, 521; Spearmint Ivan, 523; Squealing Pink Squirrel, 529; Star Cocktail,